ABER'S GONNAE GET YE!

The Billy Abercromby Story

Billy Abercromby with Fraser Kirkwood

macdonald media publishing

ABER'S GONNAE GET YE!

First published in April 2009 by **macdonald** media publishing,
22 Roxburgh Road, Paisley, PA2 0UG, Scotland
info@macdonald-media.co.uk

ISBN: 978-0-9553126-6-3
ISBN: 0-9553126-6-3

Copyright Billy Abercromby and Fraser Kirkwood 2009.

The right of Billy Abercromby and Fraser Kirkwood to be identified as authors of this work has been asserted in accordance with the Copyright, Designs and Patents Act 1988.

All rights reserved. No part of this publication may be reproduced, stored in a retrieval system, or transmitted in any form, or by any means, electronic, mechanical, photocopying, recording, or otherwise without permission in writing from the publisher.

A CIP catalogue record for this book is available from the British Library.

Design: Cameron Heggie

Printed and bound by Bell and Bain Ltd, Glasgow.

ABER'S GONNAE GET YE!

To my Mum and Dad – I owe you everything – B.A.

ABER'S GONNAE GET YE!

Contents

Foreword - By Sir Alex Ferguson C.B.E. 9

Prologue 10

1. The Magnificent Seven 13

2. Hitting The Big Time 24

3. Come And Have A Go If You Think You're Hard Enough 37

4. The Saints Go Marching In 45

5. Over Land And Sea 56

6. It's Miller Time 74

7. Always The Bridesmaid...87

8. Once… Twice... Three Times A Red Card 97

9. Broke, Busted And Disgusted... Guess Who's Back ? 103

10. The Greatest Day 114

11. The Bottle..128

12. I Fought The Law And The Law Won 139

13. Walk The Line 151

Epilogue – The Beginning Of The End…
Or The End Of The Beginning..165

Aber's Ocean's Eleven

Tony Fitzpatrick 172	Steve Clarke 185
Billy Stark 174	Jimmy Bone 187
Frank McDougall.................176	Alex Smith 189
Ricky McFarlane 178	
John McCormack 180	Derek Hamilton....................192
Lex Richardson 182	Frank McAvennie 195

Foreword

By Sir Alex Ferguson C.B.E.

Determination is a quality I have admired in people throughout my career as a manager of 35 years. In particular, when the chips are down and that person is required to call on resources maybe even unknown to himself, but that determination is buried inside them and is part of what really makes them.

Billy Abercromby has been faced with a challenge that has seen him call on this inner strength to bring himself back to a normal life. I believe that this takes not just determination, but also great courage in belief that all is not lost.

I signed Billy from his school in Maryhill about the time I started as a manager at St Mirren and immediately recognised the talent in this young lad so much that I gave him his debut when he was only 17. I remember the occasion well because when I informed him he was playing in the first team on Saturday he asked me: "What time is kick-off?" This was at a time when all kick-offs were 3.00pm. He always had a relaxed mind when it came to the game and in some ways that helped to overcome any pre-game nerves and of course he went on to have a very good career in the game.

I can only wish him well and having the wherewithal to meet this huge challenge, I am confident that he will meet that challenge.

Good luck Billy.

Sir Alex Ferguson

ABER'S GONNAE GET YE!

Prologue

IT was 2.45pm on Sunday, 5th August, 2007 – that was the day the drinking stopped. The previous day, attempts had been made by my brother Frank to get me into Stobhill Hospital in Glasgow, but I was having none of it – I wanted to watch the opening game of the SPL season at the local pub, The Inn, at Lambhill. As the Celtic-Kilmarnock game kicked off at 2pm, I sat down with a pint of Guinness and proceeded to stare at it for the next 45 minutes, oblivious to the bedlam that enveloped the pub during any game involving either of the Old Firm.

It was clear to my brother, Mark who had accompanied me, that I was having some form of physical and mental breakdown. I guess the signs were there - my skin and eyes were yellow, I had teeth like a derelict graveyard and the full ZZ Top beard. Friends called it the 'Billy Bushwhacker' look, but they were probably being too generous. My friends and family couldn't bear to look at the state of me any more and it was clear that I was in meltdown. Even when I looked in the mirror, I didn't want to admit that it was me I was looking at.

My team-mates were no longer skilled footballers, playing at the top of their profession to the delight of thousands of fans. My full-time associates were a collective of fellow alcoholics, known as the Canal Crew - after the Forth and Clyde Canal that stretches along the north of Glasgow. That's where we could be found almost every day and each of us with our own grim tale to tell.

There was a kind of dark camaraderie amongst us and each had our own nickname as though part of some Hollywood movie set in a parallel universe. There was Wee George 'Gandhi', John 'Duval', John 'Gable',

Dave 'Carey', Davie 'Carrott', Eddie 'De Niro', Radnor 'Ladd', Robin 'Banks', 'The Walrus' McPhail, John 'Motormouth' and the man only known as 'Rubber Face'. Last, but not least was part-time Canal Crew member, 'Mad Murdy', a man later known only as 'Pallet' after he dropped one on my feet, resulting in a short spell in hospital. I was known as either 'Aber' or 'Billy Bushwhacker'.

Our only shared aim was self-destruction and escape from the normal world via an endless river of alcohol. Deep down we knew it would kill us, but deep down we didn't seem to care. Some would soon be dead, whilst the rest of us often were basically the living dead.

A couple of weeks earlier, I was down on the canal side with my booze buddies as usual. I looked off to the horizon and saw the Campsie Hills. Inspired, I announced that I needed a break from this madness and decided to go on a camping holiday. Having successfully borrowed a tent and sleeping bag, I went off to get my provisions for my week-long break - two crates of sherry. I set off down the cycle path beside the canal, heading for the Campsies.

I managed to get about 500 yards, before I came across a bird-watching shelter. This'll do just fine, I thought and proceeded to unpack my belongings - the carry out - and set up the tent. I then spent the following seven days or so inside the shelter, or my tent, doing nothing but consuming my vast cargo of alcohol. Food was virtually an irrelevance. I was shuffling towards the final days of my life. Deep down I knew it and what's more – I didn't care. I remember when some passers-by saw my legs sticking out of the shelter and called for a policeman to investigate. As I lay there, utterly paralytic with booze, I could hear the policeman say: 'Ach it's only Billy – he'll be OK'. He was wrong – I had a death wish and it was on the cusp of coming true.

But back to the pub that Sunday and the state I was in. Mark - who had been sitting beside me watching the football – couldn't take any more and decided that urgent action was required. He bundled me into his car and drove at speed to Stobhill Hospital. As he presented me to the reception desk the woman behind the counter asked: 'What are you here for?' Mark's incredulous response was along the lines of: 'Take a look at him – what do you think he's here for?' A doctor was summoned and he took one look at me before announcing that I was staying. I was given several medical tests, followed by all kinds of medical paraphernalia being assembled and fitted to me. Soon the results came back:

Liver – early stages of complete failure

Kidney – almost zero function

Diabetes

Duodenal ulcer

Hiatus hernia

Blood count – 'you should be dead, Mr. Abercromby.'

To ram home the point, the doctor informed me: 'Make no mistake about this – you're one drinking binge away from death.'

Don't hold back then big chap – just give it to me straight.

But the penny had finally dropped – I was at the point of no return. If I wanted to live, I had to quit alcohol – immediately. The other option was certain death within six months – and a very painful one at that.

I chose life – but what life would I be trying to reactivate? I had lost everything that I had ever worked for, in what had been a dream career as a professional footballer. I had lost my wife, my kids, my house(s), my health, in fact everything. All I had was the support of my parents, brothers, Frank, Paul, Steven and Mark; my sister, Elaine and a handful of friends - true friends who would ensure that I would win my battles ahead. As I lay there in hospital for two weeks, the thought often crossed my mind: 'How the Hell did I get here?'

1 The Magnificent Seven

MY life began on 14th September 1958 when Glasgow factory workers Helen and William Abercromby celebrated the birth of their first-born child, William, soon shortened to Billy. No hospital bed was available in Glasgow when my mum went into labour, so she was sent to the Ross Hospital, in Paisley, where she gave birth to me. Little was she to know of the further connections to Paisley her wee baby would make in his later life! I was the first of seven children, in what turned out to be quite a sporting family. As they say in TV land - in order of appearance….

1. Myself – grew up to be a professional footballer

2. Frank – went on to be a professional boxer

3. Paul – went on to be a professional boxer

4. Brian – amateur boxer

5. Steven – a black-belt in Karate, who was also a successful kick-boxer. Later became a PC expert.

6. Elaine – the only girl and someone whom I am very, very fond of. A very caring person, who is the definition of the life and soul of the party.

7. Mark – the youngest. Went on to have a successful career as a professional footballer with Airdrie, East Fife and East Stirlingshire amongst others. Unfortunately, Mark often found himself a marked man by the referees, probably on account of his elder brother's passage through the senior game a few years previously. Sadly, Mark's career was cut short by a serious car crash.

The sporting nature of the family is clear to see and my dad, Billy senior, often told me that it was a split decision as to whether I would be a footballer or a boxer. One day, he heard Frank and me arguing in the back yard. It was a typical squabble between two young brothers in a big family.

Although there was plenty of love in the household, we didn't exactly each have toy boxes overflowing with the latest gadgets, and often the right to play with the toys of choice had to be settled with a short, sharp physical battle.

Dad called us both in to the living room and said: 'Right, enough of this nonsense! Let's sort this row out once and for all.' He reached down the side of his chair and pulled out two early Christmas presents – a football and a pair of boxing gloves. He threw them on the floor and said: 'Take your pick!' I got the ball and the rest is history.

The first sign of any promise as a footballer came at primary school, Our Lady of the Assumption, sometimes known as OLOTA. The opposition school teams used to sing 'What OLOTA rubbish' much to their amusement. But this was often shown to be a bad error of judgement as they would most likely get beaten.

In those days, I would play football in the streets with my pals from morning until night and getting selected for the school team was a big highlight. The PE Teacher was a man called Brian Blair and he played a huge part in the development of my football skills at that early age. Brian continued to take an interest in my career and I became good friends with Brian and his wife Rae long after I was established in the professional ranks.

In the modern era, much emphasis has been put upon the need to create football academies with multi-million pound state-of-the-art facilities provided to ideally create a conveyor belt of young talent. In the early 1970s, such a place did exist in Glasgow. It was St Columba Iona Secondary School, in Maryhill.

Sadly now bulldozed, my school really was a hotbed of young talent and was constantly monitored by scouts from Scotland and England to keep tabs on the young stars of the future who were constantly being produced from this wee corner of North Glasgow.

Tony Fitzpatrick, with whom I was to share almost an entire career playing beside in the St Mirren midfield, was two years ahead of me at school and I watched on with interest as he was signed by Saints' new young manager, Alex Ferguson. Jim Duffy was in my class and two years below me was a certain Charlie Nicholas.

At the school literally next door, St Augustine's, were my future Saints team-mates and legendary goalscorers, Frank McDougall and Frank McAvennie. A couple of years older, was another Saints star of the mid-

70s Fergie's Furies - John Mowat. Now people used to say that I was a bit of a hard man, but Big John was 100 per cent mental and struck fear into those trying to play against him down the wings when he was playing full-back.

I quickly found a berth in midfield of the school team and was selected for the Glasgow Schools Select. When you think about the quality of players at our school alone and then factor in the vast pool of talent across Glasgow, this was quite an achievement and my parents were filled with pride.

We went on to win the Under-15 Schoolboys' Scottish Cup and team-mates included Jim Melrose and Ian MacDonald, both of whom went on to have long and successful careers in the senior game with sides such as Greenock Morton, Partick Thistle, Celtic, and Charlton Athletic. One close friend was Hughie Donnelly, who went on to play for Aston Villa and Sunderland. Known as Shaggy on account him being an unfortunate dead ringer for Shaggy in Scooby Doo, Hughie and I still see each other regularly as he lives just a few yards up the road.

Academically, I sat my O Levels and Higher grades, gaining some creditable passes in the process. I harboured ambitions of being a PE Teacher and managed to achieve six 'O' Grades and three Highers, in Mathematics, Engineering/Drawing, and Accountancy, but sadly this fell one Higher short of the entry requirements for PE college.

This was not a massive body blow, for there was really only one way I wanted to make a career and that was as a professional footballer. John Wilson, a scout for St Mirren, lived round the corner from my parents' house in Westray Square, Milton and he persuaded me - quite easily - to sign for St Mirren Boys Club at the age of 15.

John would take me to training two nights a week after school and without his help and encouragement the future could have been so much different. Fergie had scouts like John all over the Glasgow area and was in the process of recruiting a generation of players that would go on to form the core of not just his St Mirren team, but also his hugely successful Aberdeen team. Tony Fitzpatrick, Frank McGarvey, Billy Stark, Peter Weir, Lex Richardson and many, many more young boys were brought into the senior game through Fergie's scouting operation in this era and Scottish football benefited enormously as a result.

After a short while at St Mirren Boys Club, in early May 1975 I got a message that the headmaster wanted to see me. Actually, it was a wee bit stranger than that. I was at school and heard my name being called out over the loudspeaker system. I had to go to the Headmaster's Office. 'Bloody Hell,' I thought. 'What have I done now?'

On arrival at the headmaster's office, I was ushered in to be met with the combined presence of Alex Ferguson and Bertie Auld, a member of Celtic's Lisbon Lions European Cup winning team and at the time, the manager of local senior side Partick Thistle.

Although Thistle would have been an easier commute and Bertie was a bit of a legendary figure in the Scottish game, it was Mr Ferguson who made the greater impression on me. Having already been training at Love Street with the Boys' Club and occasionally coming into contact with Fergie, I found that his sheer enthusiasm and drive bowled me over. The fact that I was born in Paisley didn't come into the equation. For the record, I am sure that Bertie wasn't smoking one of his trademark jumbo cigars as he sat in the Head's office.

Fergie said that he would like to see me at Love Street. This could only mean one of two things - I was getting a senior contract, or I was to be told that I would be freed, thus probably ending my career before it even got started. I suppose I could have gone back to Bertie Auld saying I had made a mistake, but whether a second chance would have been offered is questionable. As my dad and I headed to Love Street, I can freely admit now that I was bricking it - to use a Milton term. On arrival, we went to the Manager's Office and knocked on the door.

'Come in and sit down Billy', said Fergie. He seemed in a friendly, positive mood and my optimism rose immediately. I noticed two separate documents sitting on the table. Fergie sat in his chair, was silent for a while, then said:

'There are two contracts here, Billy. A junior contract, where you can go and play for whatever junior team you want for a couple of years, but St Mirren will keep your registration. But I also have a senior contract. Four-year deal, full-time contract. What do you think son?'

My natural disposition would be to be quite laid back about this, but the scenario in front of me was different. Here was me realising my dream of being a professional footballer. I couldn't believe it - a four-year contract. Fergie must have been impressed by what he saw and heard from the Boys' Club days.

Playing in the juniors was a non-starter – I would have been eaten alive by the hard men - and remember, I was only 17 - that populated the notoriously violent junior leagues, where fixtures between the likes of

ABER'S GONNAE GET YE!

Auchinleck Talbot and Cumnock Juniors had more in common with a re-enactment of some civil war than an actual football match. The junior teams did pay well though, but money wasn't even an issue.

In fact, without even looking at the junior contract, I picked it up and in an act of bravado that must have impressed Fergie, this bold 17-year-old lad, with his Dad at his side, simply flung it into the bin of the Manager's Office.

'Where do I sign, boss?' I asked nonchalantly. And so a 13 year Love (Street) Affair began......almost to end without me ever kicking a ball for St Mirren.

A couple of weeks later, my pal Joe Flynn and I headed off on holiday to Ladbrokes' holiday camp in Great Yarmouth to celebrate. I was later to spend plenty of time in some of Ladbrokes' more recognisable establishments, but in the mid 70s they had branched out into the world of holiday camps.

We had got some work lined up at the camp, just for a couple of weeks, to help fund our leisure activities. We were young boys down from Glasgow, mixing it with the local ladies and I was now able to tell them that they were talking to a professional footballer.

What a time we had – everything 17-year-old lads desire was available on tap (whatever way you want to interpret that). We were having so good a time that we stayed on a wee bit longer than intended. In fact, we stayed for ten weeks and so lost were we in our own private pleasure factory that we forgot to tell anyone where we were. We went away at the start of June 1975, and it was now early September. As the holidaymakers began to go home, Joe and I felt that perhaps we should do likewise. There were no more girls to chase, so I thought I'd better get home and play some football. Fergie would be cool.

I was by now seriously AWOL. The Sunday Post ran the headline 'Signed one day – he disappeared the next', as it reported the tale of how St Mirren had signed one of Glasgow's hottest young talents, only for him to promptly disappear off the face of the earth. My parents knew roughly where we were, and we phoned home occasionally, but this was before the age of mobile phones and quite often we would go wandering away from Great Yarmouth in search of fresh pleasures. It was a nightmare tracking us down. At the end of our working holiday, batteries freshly recharged as they say, I waltzed into Love Street for my first ever training session as a pro as if nothing was untoward about my sudden appearance after being posted missing. I should have reported in for pre-season training in mid-July. It was now early September. As I started to get changed, a couple of senior pros, Jackie Copland and John Young, came into the dressing room.

'Where the f**k have you been Aber?' was the greeting. 'I wouldn't bother getting changed – the Boss is going to want a word.'

Bang on cue, Fergie entered the dressing room. Silence descended.

'I see we have an extra player today', he said, sounding quite relaxed and calm. But not for long…..

With his finger pointing unwaveringly at me, he bellowed: 'You! Upstairs! Now! A word!'

I reckon that I was the first player to ever get Fergie's hairdryer treatment before ever kicking a ball for him, even in training, let alone pulling on a first team shirt. Upstairs in his office he was going crazy, ranting at me for the disappearing act.

To be fair, he had a point. I am not ashamed to admit that I was more than a little bit scared, as the man who had until that point been a firm but fair manager, often genial if truth be told, had mutated into some kind of monster right before my eyes – and I was the cause of this transformation.

His eyes narrowed to a steely stare, fixing me to the spot. His face became flushed with rage, veins bulging in his temples. The words came like a machine-gun - rapid fire, with occasional uncomfortable periods of silence as he took aim again and again:

Fergie: 'I cannot believe that you are walking around here without a care in the world. You're f*****g kidding me on son!'

'Sorry, Boss,' I reply.

'Sorry! Sorry!'

'To be honest I…'

'F*****g right you'll be honest. Where the bloody Hell have you been?'

'I got offered a job as a barman in a holiday camp. I thought it was too good a chance to refuse.'

'WHAAAAT! Too good a chance to refuse? Jesus wept - have you ANY idea what you're putting at risk?'

'Er, no.'

'I should just rip up this contract right now. But I won't. You've too much potential and I'll only be punishing myself and what bloody good is that?'

'Errrr…'

'Shut up! I should fine you for every week you were away, but I can't. I should do much worse than that, but it's against the law. So, I'm fining you the maximum two weeks' wages. If there is ever, EVER, a repeat, then you're out. Am I clear?'

'Yes boss.'

That was my punishment - fined two weeks' wages and I had only been at work for less than two minutes, never mind two weeks. I left, a chastened young man. I was under no illusion that any further steps out of line and I would be gone. In fact, it was only Fergie's belief in my abilities that allowed him to let me stay. This enhanced my desire to do my very best at all times for the man.

Looking back, it was simply an astute piece of his legendary man-management skills. When Eric Cantona was going through his troubles following the incident at Selhurst Park in the mid-90s, I could see exactly what was going on. Cantona's subsequent comeback and loyalty to Fergie after he supported the player in his time of crisis was no surprise to me – nor any other player who had ever crossed and been forgiven by the man.

Despite the less than positive start to my career at Love Street, I was soon into the swing of things. Training with the senior pros was a terrific education, although most of them were only a couple or so years older than myself. This was the side that was known as Fergie's Furies and the array of quality young players was impressive: Tony Fitzpatrick, Frank McGarvey, Derek Hyslop, Lex Richardson, Jackie Copland, Billy Stark and Bobby Reid were the mainstays of the first team.

A few seasons later, Bobby's career was cruelly cut short by injury, which was devastating not only for the big man, but for Scottish football in general – in later years, Bobby was often described as the best centre-half NOT to play for Scotland. It just goes to show what a precarious career professional football can be.

I spent most of the time learning my trade in the reserves, with other players who went on to serve the club well: Andy Dunlop, John Mowat, Bobby Torrance and Phil McAveety to name but a few. However, as at all football clubs, there was a high drop-out rate from the crop of boys signed on 'S' Forms and many didn't go on to make the grade.

Fergie was very much The Boss and ran the place from top to bottom. I wouldn't say that he ran it with fear – it was more a case of inspiring the best from players and staff with his ferocious drive and enthusiastic single-mindedness.

The club had next to no money and Fergie knew that the future lay with developing a whole team of young lads and moulding them into a force to match his own fierce ambitions. Scouting networks were established and wave after wave of trialists and 'S' forms were pitched into Paisley's very own football factory.

Only the mentally strongest would survive and go on to have a role in the club's future. You constantly had to be on your toes. Any signs of slackness – on AND off the pitch – and Fergie would crucify you.

John Mowat once had a dust-up with the boss, after he had been substituted during a game against Motherwell. Big John took his Saints top off and flung it at Fergie with the accompanying bellow of: 'And you can shove this up your arse.' (I told you that Mowat was 100% mental). Fergie went puce and barked that Big John would: 'Never kick a ball for this club again'. John rarely played for the first team again under Fergie, although he did manage some kind of brief career reprieve under different Love Street management a while later. You simply couldn't show any sign of weakness, whether in training or during matches and a lot of the young lads simply couldn't handle it. I could.

What was going on is known by some without imagination as character building, but it ran deeper than that. He was building a squad of talented young players, but turning them into men. We had to be strong to stand up to older and wiser opponents, who would be less talented; we had to forge a team spirit that would see us fight for our team-mates – sometimes literally - and we had to match the burning desire of our manager.

Fergie built a team that did all of this and this was his first big recognised success as a manager. He has gone on to become a legendary manager on the world football stage and looking at the great teams he built at Aberdeen and Manchester United, it is clear that what we experienced at Love Street was the prototype for the methodology Sir Alex used creating exciting sides that could also fight their corner when required.

He was a superb motivator and instilled a belief in him from his players, that we would follow him over the cliff if so required. A feeling of 'us against the world' was fostered and eagerly practised by the playing staff.

The definition of 'the rest of the world' basically meant anyone not involved in the playing or coaching staff.

Even St Mirren directors were not welcomed into the fold and at one stage Fergie even had a sign outside the dressing room door, saying 'No Directors Allowed'. This was to be prophetic and the role of St Mirren's directors over the coming years in relation to meddling with the coaching staff was quite astonishing. But more of that later.

Prior to the start of 1976-1977, St Mirren embarked on a Caribbean Tour, organised by club director Yule Craig (they weren't all bad). Not long out of school in Possil, I found myself flying to the other side of the world being paid to play football beside the crystal blue waters of the Caribbean. To think that 12 months previously I almost blew it by going on an extended break to Great Yarmouth.

It was a fantastic trip and went a long way to further cementing the team spirit and gang mentality that Fergie was purposefully generating. In one game, the boss put me on as a first half sub. I was thrilled. Ten minutes later, it was clear that Fergie was less than thrilled, when he subbed me. I was astonished, but it was clear what the problem was.

'Billy – one of the things you are allowed to do in football is run,' Fergie says to me. 'You'll find it helps. What the f**k was going on out there?'

He was right – as he always is. This 17-year old from Possil had simply been walking about in the 100-degree heat – I couldn't run as this was a culture shock too far.

Despite this, the boss kept the faith in me and we headed off to Guyana for the next game, unaware of the mayhem about to ensue. The locals had turned out in force, probably in the hope of seeing their boys give these Big Time Charlies - despite the fact that we were still in Scottish Division 1 - a boot up the backside. The baying crowd were kept back from the pitch by a six-feet high chicken wire fence, but were still very, very close to the action.

This action basically involved the local team kicking lumps out of the sunburnt superstars from far off, glamorous Paisley. After one particularly brutal foul, the boss decided to make a change. He put himself on and all Hell really was about to break loose.

Fergie had only retired from playing a couple of years earlier and was still fit. He was also still well-versed in the dark arts of an aggressive centre-forward and the local hard man was about to rue the error of his ways.

Within minutes, Fergie had bulldozed this guy, not once, but twice – the latter would have been classified as a knockout win. Red carded, the boss trudged off – mission accomplished. And this was supposed to have been a friendly.

In the changing room afterwards, we were still in shock, awe and not a little admiration at what we had just witnessed. Someone had tried to sort out one of his boys and Fergie had taken the retribution personally. This was a quite extraordinary managerial technique at work.

Fergie broke the silence: 'Nobody and I mean NOBODY, will ever mention this happened. Right?' We never did – not after what we'd just seen.

One other memory of the Caribbean trip was experiencing Fergie's sharp financial acumen. One day in the West Indies I had seen a diver's watch that took my fancy. God knows why, as there was little chance of me developing a sub-aqua hobby in the River Clyde in mid-70s Glasgow.

I didn't have my wallet on me, but Fergie did and offered to buy the watch, on the basis that we settled up when we got home. Back in Paisley, I gave Fergie the required £25 for the watch, only to find out a few days later that it actually cost only £15. Did I have the bottle to ask for the £10? Colleagues and opponents will testify that on the park losing my bottle was never an option. However, this was the only occasion when my nerve went – but I'd challenge any 17-year old to take on Fergie over a disputed tenner.

The 1976-1977 season saw the fruition of Fergie's plans, as Fergie's Furies swept to the First Division title, playing some fantastic attacking football on the way. The local public were swept along and crowds swelled massively as the season wore on.

In January 1977, St Mirren swept aside Premier League Dundee United 4-1 in the Scottish Cup 3rd Round, before losing out 2-1 away to Motherwell. Over 10,000 fans travelled to Motherwell to see Saints kicked out of the cup – literally.

Fergie's furious reaction to the refereeing that day seemed to help us redouble the efforts to get promoted. Finally, I got the chance to play and on March 8th 1977 I made my first team debut against St Johnstone, in a 1-1 draw.

I went on to make a couple of substitute appearances, but that was my only taste of the action during that historic season. I spent the year learning my trade in the reserves, with over 30 appearances for the Second Eleven.

As the first team went on a charge to the First Division title, I was a peripheral figure, very much looking in from the outside. I was never taken to away games, and didn't mix too much with the first team boys. But little was I to know that Fergie had been keeping tabs on my progress and that next season was to suddenly see my emergence and the real beginning of my professional career.

2 Hitting The Big Time

ST MIRREN were in the Premier League for the first time in the club's history. Most teams or managers would probably set their sights on survival, but Fergie was having none of that. He was aiming higher: he publicly stated that we were aiming for the title.

This sort of sabre-rattling was music to the ears of the Paisley public, who were very much on board the Fergie Rollercoaster. This was the era when he famously used to be driven around Paisley on match day mornings, using a loudhailer to whip up the masses and get them down to Love Street.

For the players, this was superb man-management. We believed in this man and if he felt that we were that good, then we felt ten-feet tall and ready to take on anyone.

One of his tricks was to get his assistant manager Davie Provan and physio Ricky McFarlane to hold him back in true pantomime style, as he tried to get to some hapless referee at the half-time break. At the time, we didn't know it was an act, but we would sit there mouths agape, until Fergie came in and still in full flight would fire us up with verve and passion to carry out his commandments. What he said was written in stone and we followed it to the letter – or at least tried to.

August 13th 1977 saw Saints play their first ever Premier League match - a 1-1 draw at Love Street with Clydebank, who were our title rivals from the previous season.

I played from the start and went on to make over 30 appearances that season in the first-team. This was a big surprise to many, seeing as how I had featured so little the previous season, but I believe that Fergie had been getting me ready for this top-flight campaign and I was gladly going to take the chance he had given me.

The plan was to keep playing our brand of exciting, attractive football, whilst aiming to immediately break into the top echelons of the league.

Privately, Fergie was simply aiming to keep Saints up in that first season, without compromising his football principles. This was achieved, although we came close to sinking in the last quarter of the season.

At the end of March, a crucial late goal by Frank McGarvey at Somerset Park saw us edge a 1-0 victory against Ayr United - fellow candidates for the drop. In the following seven games we only managed a handful of points, but just managed to stay up. Looking at the subsequent fortunes of the two clubs - Ayr United have never been in the Premier League since - that season was era-defining for St Mirren Football Club.

This could also be said of some of the fixtures that season threw up. We beat Celtic TWICE at Parkhead in the league, a feat thought about as likely as Lord Lucan signing for the Buddies.

We also entered the Anglo-Scottish Cup , beating Fulham and Notts County, before losing 3-2 on aggregate to Bristol City in the Final in late 1977. In the Fulham game I found myself on the same pitch as the legendary George Best, less than 18 months after signing from school.

It wouldn't be the last time that George would grace the Love Street turf. He was in the twilight of his English league career, but was still a huge draw as a bumper crowd turned up in driving rain at Love Street to see us win 5-3 on the night in a wonderful game of football.

George levelled the tie at 3-3 with about ten minutes to go, only for goals from myself, then Brian Docherty, to seal the tie in an incredible 90 minutes. The first leg 1-1 draw in London had served notice to everyone that Saints were a team on the up and the victory in Paisley was no mean feat.

In the first leg of the final I scored Saints' only goal as we were beaten 2-1 by Bristol City, in Paisley. A 1-1 draw at Ashton Gate, with Bobby Reid scoring for Saints, was not enough.

We were the first Scottish team to get to the final and sweet revenge would be ours a couple of years later. The away trips to the English clubs were a welcome distraction from domestic issues and helped increase my burgeoning football education at Love Street. It might not have been the most glamorous tournament in the world, but I loved it.

It was also St Mirren's centenary year and a special match for The Centenary Cup was organised to commemorate the event. The opponents were beyond the expectations of all Saints fans - and players.

ABER'S GONNAE GET YE!

Reigning European Champions, Liverpool came to Love Street on Monday 12th December 1977. What a team they brought: Ray Clemence, Tommy Smith, Phil Neal, Phil Thompson, Ray Kennedy, Emlyn Hughes, Terry McDermott, Steve Heighway, David Fairclough, Ian Callaghan, Jimmy Case, David Johnson, Alan Hansen and last, but not least, King Kenny Dalglish. This was as good as it got in European or World football.

The Saints team was a bit more modest when it came to household names:

Ally Hunter, John Young, Alex Beckett, Tony Fitzpatrick, Bobby Reid, Jackie Copland, Derek Hyslop, Lex Richardson, Billy Stark, Frank McGarvey, Ian Munro, Andy Dunlop and yours truly.

We were 1-0 down to a Kenny Dalglish goal with two minutes to go when a cross-cum-shot was fired across the face of the box and I slid it in from six yards to equalize. I didn't score many goals, but this was my all-time favourite. Love Street went berserk.

This might have only been a friendly, but it was being played in a competitive manner and the sheer glamour of the opposition lent the game a lot of importance to the 20,000 locals who packed the stadium.

The game was drawn 1-1 and we immediately had a penalty shoot-out to determine the winner. Liverpool ran-out 5-4 winners on spot-kicks. I got to take one and thankfully scored from the penalty spot but only just. I sclaffed the ball from the spot, but still managed to nutmeg Ray Clemence. I was in good company as Kenny Dalglish did the same thing to Clemence - albeit not from the penalty spot - at Hampden Park in 1976, to the delight of an entire Scottish nation.

That season saw Fergie create a solid, regular midfield four of Tony Fitzpatrick, Billy Stark, Lex Richardson and myself. Fitzy was often referred to as The Train on account of the non-stop running and energetic style he had. Some players are described as having a good engine, but Fitzy had a three-litre injection model.

Just watching him was inspiring and he was a terrific motivator – no wonder that Fergie made him captain before he was 21. If I thought the ball was going out, I was prone to thinking 'f**k that for a game of soldiers' and let it run out. On the other hand, Tony would run and chase down every lost cause and this soon rubbed off on me. Allied to his work rate, he was a superb passer of the ball and was great at bringing others into play and switching directions of attack with one clever pass after another.

Billy Stark was a gentleman. A quiet lad from Anniesland, in Glasgow, Billy was a man of few words, but when he spoke you listened. It is no surprise that he is becoming a respected coach in his own right these days. A genius of a player and a scorer of many important goals. Nicknamed Starsky, he was also rather unkindly given another moniker - The Pike. I always thought this was a bit unfair, but some of the boys reckoned he looked like the fish with a hook in its mouth.

Lex Richardson – my room-mate and fellow night-time adventurer. Lex was about five years older than me, but had come straight from the tough junior football ranks – a sure-fire way of turning a boy into a man. Tough in the tackle, Lex also loved to attack down the left flank and in many ways was a complete player.

Tony, Billy and Lex had formed a three-man attacking midfield during the all-out cavalier style of the '76-'77 promotion-winning team. Looking back, it is possible that Fergie wanted to be a wee bit more pragmatic for the Premier League and opted for a 4-4-2. The fourth man was to be me and this Gang of Four was to prove the cornerstone for the St Mirren team for some years to come.

Many successful sides are built on a solid back four, but without blowing my own trumpet, the St Mirren sides of '77 to the mid 80s were built around a dynamic midfield. We each seemed to know where each other was and played almost telepathically - very occasionally having moments of playing pathetically as well.

Tony, Billy and Lex would still form the attacking roles and my job was to provide a defensive edge to the midfield flair. I was more than happy to do this and thrived on the challenge. The boys used to say that if I crossed the half-way line I would need a map to get back into my own half, but I still managed to chip in with the odd goal – usually as the result of a (very) late run.

My arrival in the box was usually a complete surprise to both the opposition and my team-mates, so I guess I had the element of surprise. It also gave me close-up experience at a young age of seeing the real mechanics behind a successful midfield. Every time one of the boys attacked, one of us would fill-in as cover; every time one of us needed a target for a pass, one of us would be available. It was fluid, exciting and successful – Fergie's midfield blueprint would be maintained at Love Street for years to come.

ABER'S GONNAE GET YE!

One of the most crucial Fergie signings was Jimmy Bone who had been playing for Arbroath. Papa, as he was known, even then was classed as a veteran striker having played for Partick Thistle, Celtic, Norwich City and Toronto Blizzard.

Expectations of Jimmy, who had been around the block more times than a dodgy second hand car, were limited, but what a signing he was to be – on AND off the pitch. Papa was a fanatical trainer and this probably explained the longevity of his career and this was a living example to the rest of us. More than that, Jimmy was the life and soul of the party, always playing practical jokes and doing anything to raise morale. Frank McAvennie may disagree, as he once had his jockstrap liberally coated in Deep Heat by Jimmy, with the inevitable results.

Other than his life as social convenor, Jimmy seemed to thrive at Love Street and on the pitch he was a handful for opposing defenders. The individual highlight of his playing days at Love Street was his amazing solo goal versus Aberdeen in a 1-1 draw at Love Street in 1981. It won the BBC's Goal of the Season award that year – and deservedly so. Jimmy got the ball just inside his own half, turned and set off at pace in the direction of Jim Leighton's goal at the Love Street end. With a combination of strength and skill, he bulldozed past Willie Miller and Doug Rougvie (and that in itself was no mean feat), before ending his 60 yard run by shooting past Leighton. By this time, the rest of us had stopped playing and just watched on as Jimmy started to build up a head of steam – the chances of him passing the ball were minimal at best.

Jimmy was eventually made captain, following the sale of Tony Fitzpatrick to Bristol City in July 1979 for £250,000, but Tony would return a couple of years later from Bristol without a West Country accent and combine with Jimmy and the rest of us to greater glories – but more of that later.

Today - and I am not just talking about St Mirren - I am saddened at the lack of characters in the game. It looks like all the youngsters have the individuality on and off the pitch coached out of them.

Back in my day - cue the brass band playing the Hovis advert tune - the game was full of characters and that applies to exponents of both skill and, how could you put it, the defensive aspect of the game.

The pace of the game was slower and the skill of a footballer flourished – despite the much more violent tackling that was commonplace. It was almost like watching good triumph over evil for fans, as they watched their team's skilful players try to outdo the assassins of the opposition.

Today, there seems to be much more emphasis on not losing, as opposed to trying to win, with teams playing identical systems, with basically identical players, at 100 miles per hour.

When he was manager of St Mirren in the late 80s early 90s, Tony Fitzpatrick echoed the above opinion in a BBC interview following St Mirren's 3-0 win at Parkhead. He said that he had to leave flair players out of certain games, claiming that the Premier League was starting to demand 'a different kind of beast'. Tony was right and sadly, bar the odd exception, not much has changed.

It had been a tough year the previous season, playing almost exclusively in the reserves whilst the rest of the squad went on to win the league, but here we were in the big time and the manager had selected me as a first-choice midfielder and an obvious key part of his plans.

You knew that your place was never guaranteed under Fergie and the incentive to keep playing well to retain your berth was always high. Something must have worked well though, as this midfield four would remain very much in the forefront of St Mirren team selections for the next five years (Fitzy's brief hiatus at Bristol City notwithstanding).

As the season ended, an astonishing chain of events unfolded that resulted in the sacking of Alex Ferguson. Even to this day, the Paisley public still shake their heads in disbelief at this and I know that the supporters still feel some kind of embarrassment at the association St Mirren has with this piece of footballing history.

Fergie had long had a frosty to non-existent relationship with club chairman, Willie Todd and vice-chairman, John Corson, with all parties set on collision course for months. This was despite, or to be more accurate because of, our great success in the previous two years. Fergie was basically running the club from top-to-bottom and the players and staff would listen to him above anyone else – on any given matter.

This grated with Todd and Corson, who would regularly have what is known as a frank exchange of views with Fergie at the regular board meetings. All this succeeded in doing was widening the gap between the parties. In addition, it was widely felt that Todd and Corson - especially the former - were keen to bask in the limelight created by Fergie's efforts. This went down like a knackered lift with Ferguson. As players, we weren't involved in any of this, but at a club as small as St Mirren, it was impossible not to know there was trouble brewing behind the scenes.

In retrospect, it was clear that Fergie had been "made aware" that Aberdeen were keen on him taking over at Pittodrie, following Billy McNeill's move to the managerial position at Celtic. Jock Stein had just been offered the post of managing the Celtic pools – showing that St Mirren didn't have a monopoly on maniacal boardroom decision-making.

This was the time that directors should have been making their peace with Fergie and building a partnership with him for the future. It is possible that Fergie was looking for some kind of assurances that St Mirren would back his ruthlessly ambitious plans for maintaining the astonishing development that had been achieved so far.

Not so, however, and Fergie was sacked. Apparently for umpteen breaches of contract, including attending the Liverpool v. Bruges 1978 European Cup Final, at Wembley without permission of the Directors. Fergie took St Mirren to an Industrial Tribunal, but lost the case. This cast another shadow over the whole sorry saga for both Fergie and St Mirren.

However, the seeds of the club's future success had been sown and a new manager was on the horizon. As players, we weren't happy at Fergie's exit – to a man we almost idolised him, but we were still wise enough to know that life must go on and we still had our own careers to concentrate on.

It was important that we didn't lose any momentum and got a manager in who would see to this and recruit some new faces to further strengthen the squad to see us progress. To be fair the board didn't hang around too long and the imposing figure of Jim Clunie was soon appointed as the new manager of St Mirren.

My main concern was that my professional career was just really taking off and I loved being at St Mirren. But would the new boss rate me? I soon realised that these fears were unnecessary.

Big Jim was an ex-St Mirren player. A no-nonsense old school centre-half, I am led to believe, and he did play in the club's last major trophy win - at that time - the 1959 Scottish Cup Final although he was playing for Aberdeen!

He came to manage St Mirren from Southampton, where he had a very successful role as assistant to Lawrie McMenemy, especially their famous 1976 FA Cup win against Manchester United. However, the lure of coming home and leaving one set of Saints to take over as boss at the other, was too much to turn down I suppose.

The other attraction was that Fergie had left St Mirren in a great position, with a talented, driven squad and the club was very much on the up. If someone could add to that squad and keep the blend that had been developing, then they would be on to a good thing. Big Jim wasn't daft.

Some great players and characters were either brought in, or developed through the ranks, in the same fashion as myself. Ricky McFarlane, one of the nicest guys you could hope to meet, was physio during Fergie's era, but had a large part in helping develop the young lads at the club, including myself.

When Jim Clunie arrived, Ricky was appointed assistant manager and had an even greater influence on the team. Jim's team-talks tended to be rather unelaborate and it was Ricky who would give out the in-depth tactical roles and ideas to the players.

He always used to take me to one side and go through a very serious, detailed five-minute briefing of what the game plan was to be. He did this with all the players, but seemed to find it difficult with me, for at the end of every speech, he would pause, roll his eyes and say 'Och, just go and do what you do Aber - but if you're going to do something stupid, DON'T GET CAUGHT!'

A really strong squad was being created and the nucleus of the Fergie team was still in place. In came goalkeeper Billy Thomson, from Partick Thistle. Billy was a local lad from Linwood and would quickly become arguably the best keeper in Scotland. He was so reliable that you always had confidence playing in front of him. He was also a handsome big bastard, with Scandinavian looks that didn't quite seem in keeping with his Renfrewshire roots!

The fact that he only got a handful of Scotland caps was partly down to Alan Rough's good form, but probably down to the fact that if you played for a small provincial team like St Mirren, then you really didn't get a look-in at international level.

In the late 70s and early 80s, Billy was clearly the best and most consistent young keeper in Scotland, yet his lack of Scotland caps was a disgrace. I was very friendly with Billy and his family and he was not only a superb colleague, but a great friend.

Alex Beckett and Iain Munro were our settled full-back combination, very different in style to each other, but extremely effective. Becky had no

ABER'S GONNAE GET YE!

fear whatsoever and would run through the proverbial brick wall if required. Those on the end of his strong/brutal tackling would probably have preferred if he had run at a brick wall instead of them and he was a fearsome opponent for wingers across the land.

Iain 'Mini' Munro was a supremely talented full-back and had been signed by Fergie in the early stages of 77-78 in a bid to improve the experience and ability of the squad in the first season in the Premier League.

It was Iain's second spell at Love Street and he seemed to thrive even after Fergie's departure. Iain went on to win seven Scotland caps while at Love Street – a magnificent achievement. As well as being a sound defender, his attacking abilities were superb and he was for a period of time our No. 1 penalty taker – provided we actually got some!

Iain fell-out with the club over some contractual issues and left in the 1980 close season, but his place was more than ably taken by John Young, who probably thought that his first team days were over by then. John was a great guy, with loads of experience and his Indian summer at St Mirren went on for a few years after he signed on at Love Street.

Big Jackie Copland was still at the heart of the defence and as Bobby Reid struggled with chronic injuries as mentioned earlier, it was the imposing figure and haircut of Andy 'Harpo' Dunlop who was partnering him. Andy was a solid centre-half who knew his limitations and played around them – in other words, he knew what he did well and focused on that. In all good teams there is a thread of simplicity – get people in who know their jobs and know how to do them well. Andy fitted that bill as a no-nonsense stopper.

Local youngster Mark Fulton, from Kilbarchan, was also forcing his way into the first team as a very promising centre-half. A tall, good-looking lad, Mark definitely fancied himself on the ball, that's for sure. I'm sure he thought he was the next Beckenbauer and although he could be ferocious in the tackle and solid in the air, my abiding memories of Mark were his endlessly frustrating habit of taking too long on the ball, as if he was saying 'look at me before I make this great pass'. Nonetheless, Mark would go on to have a key role at the heart of the defence for several years and as time wore on he became a valued team-mate.

The main issue I had with Mark was that it appeared to me that he seemed to think he was above us, or more accurately, above The Gang that populated a corner of the dressing room for many years. The membership would change occasionally, but over time this executive club included Fitzy, Lex, Jimmy Bone, Frank MacDougall, Frank McAvennie, Brian Gallagher and Derek Hamilton. A Rogues' Gallery? Not even close! However, despite our obvious faults, the gang mentality did serve St Mirren very well throughout the 70s and 80s.

I cannot forget to mention one of the main men of our gang - Frank McGarvey was still up front and making a real name for himself as a goal-getting striker, with an excellent touch and good vision at bringing others into the game… eventually.

Frank never seemed to believe in beating a man once, when it could be done three times, which suited me, as my (very) late runs to the opposition penalty area meant that I would be on the receiving end of one of Frank's killer passes. This is a polite way of saying that he had beaten his man three times and was now ready to find a team-mate.

He was known in the dressing room as Elmer - he'll kill me for mentioning that nickname - and I had a love/hate relationship with him, For all the years we played together, or even as opponents, we always seemed to bring out the worst/best in each other. Deep down though, I think there was enormous mutual respect and I have nothing but admiration for Frank as a friend and colleague. Frank was a great exponent of one-liners and put-downs that could cut someone to pieces in the midst of an argument. He was never short of an opinion – and he was always right of course.

In May 1979, Frank was sold to Liverpool for a massive fee of £300,000 - Dalglish had been signed for a then record £440,000 less than two years previously. It was a huge step-up for Frank and in retrospect it may have been too big a move for him.

Liverpool were the Kings of English and European football and this was a totally different concept to playing for the band of brothers at little old Love Street. Saying that, if Liverpool had come in for me, then I would have probably signed up as well. Despite appearing in the 1979 Charity Shield, Frank never really made an impact at Anfield and signed for Celtic in March 1980. Frank came back to Love Street in 1985 and was to reunite with Fitzy, Jimmy and myself for a few more great days at Love Street - and Hampden Park.

As Frank left in the summer of 1979, the club bought in two strikers –

Frank loves that – it needed two to replace him - and these two were to become among the most lethal in Scotland, giving Saints the cutting edge that was missing if we were to truly challenge for honours.

Doug Somner arrived from Partick Thistle and immediately became a veritable goal machine, with 25 league goals from 32 starts being his haul in the first season.

Did he play for Scotland, or even get in a squad? Don't be silly. The following season carried on in a similar vein, until Doug got an injury from which he never really recovered and his career at Love Street ended prematurely – a great shame for all concerned and his tally of 32 goals in 61 league matches has meant that he has always been kept in high regard by the St Mirren fans.

There used to be a badge in the club shop that said 'Jesus Saves – but Somner nets the rebound!' and that kind of sums up the affection with which the man was held. The other notable fact about Doug's scoring record was that he didn't bloat the statistics by scoring bags of goals against lesser teams. Doug had the knack of scoring crucial goals, often the deciding goal in a narrow win and this was invaluable for the team's progress. Not to put too fine a point on it, you could always rely on Doug to pull you out the sh**e – as I am sure the late Jim Clunie would have put it.

The other big signing was my old pal from Possil, Frank MacDougall. Frank had been doing very well for himself as a prodigious striker at Clydebank and the race was on between St Mirren and Celtic for his signature. The fabled biscuit tin must have been truly glued down at Parkhead, for it was St Mirren who won the race and signed the big man for a then record fee between two Scottish clubs of £150,000.

Frank didn't have the same explosive impact of Doug Somner and competition for places between Doug, Jimmy and Frank kept them all on their toes – in much the same way the midfield area had been for yours truly for a few seasons already. A man of few words, Frank always looked very serious and allied to his physical presence, he was thought of as a bit of a hard man striker – a rare breed. In truth, Frank was a very funny guy, although often unintentionally.

He earned the nickname 'Luther' among the players as a result of him trying to voice his views during a Jim Clunie team talk before a game with Watford: probably fresh from watching Bob Wilson on Football Focus,

Frank called out: 'Hey Boss - we'll need to watch out for that Luther Blizzard'. He was being serious. And for those who don't know, he should have said Luther Blisset, the Watford, AC Milan and England striker.

In February 1980, Frank suffered a serious leg break after a tackle from Danny McGrain in a match at Love Street against Celtic that ruled him out for the rest of the season. I think I was suspended for this match (no surprises there then) and I recall it being a truly terrible tackle.

Big Frank was to show his true strength in returning early the next season better than ever and went on to be a central part of the Saints' strikeforce, scoring many memorable and important goals in the process, with Saints' supporters nicknaming him 'Zico' after the Brazilian superstar footballer.

In my opinion he was the deadliest finisher that I played with, purely on a chances to goals ratio and bearing in mind some of the strikers that I played with (McGarvey, Somner and McAvennie) this is some compliment. Frank was signed by Fergie at Aberdeen in 1985 and went on to win the European Golden Boot until a serious spinal injury forced him to retire in his prime as a footballer.

Another key striker on the staff in this era was Alan Logan - a lightning quick lad with a sharp eye for any chances in the six-yard box. Alshie was always going to struggle to break into the team with such a strong group of strikers already at the club, but bizarrely it was his initial successful burst onto the first team scene that was arguably his undoing at Love Street.

Alan came on as a sub in a game against Partick Thistle at Love Street, with us trailing 2-0 at the break. Forty-five minutes later and St Mirren had run out 3-2 winners, with Alan netting a hat-trick. Immediately tagged as supersub, it was a label that would haunt him, as he struggled to break into the squad past the likes of Somner, McDougall and McAvennie and found himself on the bench for most of the time. The more he made an impact from the bench, the more it seemed to vindicate decisions to play him from there – he was Supersub after all.

Alan got a really bad injury that almost forced him out of the game and he was never the same again. He finally left Saints for Partick Thistle in part of the deal that brought Kenny McDowall to the club, but Alan's impact at Love Street will be fondly remembered by all who saw him play.

On the wing was Peter Weir. What a talent. Again, a local boy, born in Johnstone and signed from Neilston Juniors, Peter had it all for a winger. He could beat a man with ease and had a great range of passing and crossing. How good was Peter? He got four of his six Scotland caps while at Love Street and this meant Peter was very, very good.

'The Sink', as he was known on account of the amount of Tennent's lager he could hold, was the best two-footed player I ever played with. And although he played mainly on the left-wing, this level of natural skill meant that he was always confusing defenders. A genius. Jimmy Bone, Doug Somner and Frank MacDougall thrived on his service and soon we thought that we really did have a chance of winning honours.

This was a really good squad and we felt that progress was being made. As a unit we worked well together and fought for each other.

Off the pitch, another significant development in my life had been achieved - I had got married. I had known Anne-Marie since we were at school, so although many thought we were on the young side to get married at 20 years of age, the pair of us were inseparable and the living image of love's young dream.

Following our marriage in November 1978 we moved into our first house together in Howard Street, Paisley - next door to Billy Thomson, the St Mirren keeper. I bought the house from Tony Fitzpatrick, who had got married only two years previously. But it wasn't long before we sold that home and moved to another house in Cross Road, Paisley followed by a move to the village of Lochwinnoch in the heart of the beautiful Renfrewshire countryside. A long way from the back streets of Possil and a good marker of the successful career I was carving for myself as a professional footballer.

3 Come And Have A Go If You Think You're Hard Enough

MY basic role as a footballer was simple. First, win the ball and then give it to the players who can really do the – footballing - damage. A wise man once said that there is no point in being a ball-winner unless you know what to do with it. I prided myself on my passing ability, although this was often overlooked in lieu of the more aggressive style of my play. What counts is the opinion of my former team-mates and managers and I know that my distribution ability was appreciated by one and all.

I loved this passing side of the game and as I got more experienced so my skills in this area grew. I used to know before I even made a tackle what I was going to do with the ball – I had the pass already worked out. These quick switches in the pattern of play from defence to attack are vital to any team's success, just as much as the goals from the glamour boys up front and I gained enormous satisfaction perfecting this art.

The other element of midfield combat that I mastered and became my most publicly recognised asset, was the knack of coming out on top in fairly brutal exchanges with opponents. 50/50? I preferred 40/60 against my favour – at least it gave the opposition a chance. Future team-mate Brian Gallagher once told me that he used to go and watch St Mirren in those days and admire, from the perspective of a fellow pro, my speciality of letting an opponent have some space, then quickly let him get close to me.

This is quite an easy trick, as you basically track back at the same speed as the attacking opponent, then stop sharply. The opponent is on top of you before they realise it, and you - the defender - can quickly go into the tackle winning the ball and taking out the man – without conceding a foul.

ABER'S GONNAE GET YE!

Soon my reputation was spreading among opposition fans, players, coaches, managers and of course, referees. The abuse from fans at away grounds didn't bother me one iota – I loved it. It meant that I was getting to them and this meant that St Mirren were getting to them. They didn't seem to approve.

I lost count of the number of opponents who used to shout their mouths off by way of attempted intimidation. 'I'm gonnae f*****g do you Aber!'

'Oh yeah?'

Mouthing off wasn't my style. Actions tend to speak a lot louder than words. Delivering the message in silence seemed to increase its effectiveness – it certainly shut up a few of the gobby opponents who stupidly tried to intimidate me with their empty threats.

The only way I could be nullified was to do me – and NOBODY ever managed that. As for the refs, I became friendly with a Grade 1 ref - he'll have to remain nameless to preserve his innocence - who told me that at the occasional referee meetings, when it came to St Mirren the unanimous view was that they should keep an eye on Abercromby. But they still couldn't stop me 99 per cent of the time. To paraphrase my hero Mohammed Ali: 'Float like a butterfly….. sting like a bee… you'll never stop me….. I'm Abercromby !'

I learned that the then Dundee United manager, Jim McLean used to put up a picture of me on the wall of the home dressing room at Tannadice when his team were to play Saints. The intention was to get his boys fired up and 'stop this bastard'. I'll take that as the compliment it was undoubtedly intended by the grumpy sod. In the end, it was a vision of me holding a major trophy that would help send his blood pressure into meltdown.

What I do know is that the St Mirren fans were certainly appreciative and this would often appear in the form a chant coming from the Buddies support, that was to go down in St Mirren folklore as my calling card.

In the late 70s and early 80s, Celtic's ball-winning midfielder, Roy Aitken, nicknamed Shirley Temple or The Bear - depending on how brave you were - used to patrol Celtic's midfield with an air of menace. 'The Bear is gonnae get ye!' was the song from Celtic fans, but this soon turned into 'Feed The Bear! Feed The Bear!' and Roy usually didn't have to wait too long for his next meal.

'Aber's gonnae get ye! Aber's gonnae get ye!' - the re-working of the Aitken chant, but sung with more passion and menace, started to emanate from the St Mirren support at games in the early 80s and got more and more popular as the years went on.

It was like a call-to-arms and I almost felt obliged to give them the victim they seemed to crave. I knew they would be disappointed if I didn't give them a body or two in the 90 minutes.

From speaking to a few St Mirren fans over the years about this song, it was clear that I was not far off the mark in my assumptions. They saw me as St Mirren's answer to Dirty Harry – a maverick who would bend the rules to right the wrongs given out to the Saints players on the pitch.

That all sounds a wee bit dramatic to me, but one of my main roles was to ensure that we competed in midfield and that no quarter was given. I had a responsibility to protect some of our younger and flair players from the intimidatory tactics that would come their way. Fight fire with fire was my thinking and the Saints fans just loved it. I'll freely admit it – I'd have kicked my Granny to get the points for St Mirren.

As teams became more aware of my reputation, I found myself the target for even more abuse from opposition fans and some misguided attempts by opposition players to take me out – no doubt under instructions from their respective managers.

However, I must have been privately acknowledged and respected by some of the managers – bar Jim McLean, of course - and in 1985 Celtic made me aware of their intention to sign me to replace Mark Reid, who had just joined Charlton Athletic. For one reason or another, the deal never went through and I certainly have no regrets – St Mirren was such a big part of me that leaving would have been a massive wrench – regardless of the obvious attractions of joining a massive club like Celtic.

Ironically, instead of St Mirren selling me to Celtic in the summer of 1985, we ended up signing Frank McGarvey from Celtic, with Frank returning to Saints just in time to achieve what he described as his greatest success in the game.

A few years after I finished playing, a young reserve goalkeeper from my final days at Love Street, John Hillcoat, accurately summed up my reputation during my playing days in a couple of articles he did for the

ABER'S GONNAE GET YE!

Sunday Mail:

"Every team needs a silent assassin - a figure who can intimidate the opposition before he even steps out on to the pitch. The first player I can remember who sent a shiver down spines across Scotland was St Mirren legend Billy Abercromby. I was just a scrawny teenager when I first met the bold Aber and he had a fearsome reputation. I had built up a mental picture of a guy who was eight feet tall and could put you in a headlock and hold you until you fell unconscious. In reality the Scottish Cup-winning skipper was much smaller but Billy battled as if he was Paisley's answer to William Wallace."

And….

"There's one former player who easily matched fearsome Souness in the bone-crunching stakes. Step forward St Mirren's Scottish Cup-winning captain Billy Abercromby. Players during the 70s and 80s feared Aber because they knew the midfielder was always ready to dish out some belters. Even in training the hard man would be up to his tricks like standing on team-mates' fingers as they hit the deck after one of his "enthusiastic" tackles. And long before Bobo Balde had a song in his honour, Saints fans used Aber's style of play to intimidate the opposition. Every time a rival player got the ball the Love Street faithful would chant, "Aber's gonnae get ye" as if he was St Mirren's version of the bogeyman."

This was very accurately observed by 'Hilly', who was just a boy living in Linwood in the mid 80s when I would pick him up for training. I must point out though – I would never stand on a colleagues hands….well maybe not those of the goalies.

'Hilly' used to travel with me when we were both at Dunfermline later in our careers. The journey usually involved crossing the Forth Road Bridge and more to the point, waiting for ages to get through the queues at the toll booths. One afternoon we were at the back of the queue when I looked in the rear view mirror and saw a car heading for us at great speed. It certainly wasn't going to stop in time. I managed to pull my car just slightly to the side, before……

'Watch it Hilly…..' CRAAAAAAASH!

Turns out the driver was a North Sea diver, who was coming back home after a shift on the rigs. He had fallen asleep at the wheel and only my moving our car at a slight angle had stopped us from being killed by his runaway car. Scottish journalism owes me a favour.

Of course, my style of play meant that I came into close contact with some of the hard men of Scottish and British football through my career

ABER'S GONNAE GET YE!

and I have often been asked as to who was the toughest guy that I came up against. There were plenty who took a sly kick at me, or mouthed off the empty threats, but there were some who were genuinely competitive and hard as nails. My Top 10 Hard Men would be -

(cue "Top of the Pops" theme tune)

10. Doug Rougvie – Aberdeen's gigantic full-back. Doug was a scary looking guy. Apparently as nice as ninepence off the pitch, but a totally different proposition on it. Coming across like some kind of zombie on steroids, Doug struck fear into anyone coming up against him down Aberdeen's flank. Not me though – I loved the challenge and the contests were very much in the mould of David v. Goliath. I think there was certainly an element of mutual respect, as year after year we used to throw ourselves into some serious collisions, much to the amusement of team-mates and fans of both sides.

9. Roy Aitken – He was a great guy. Never purposefully dirty, just completely crazy. He was some kind of totem figure in the Celtic midfield and the view was that if you could topple Big Roy, then a message would be sent to the rest of the Celtic team. Guess who got the job of delivering the message?

8. Kenny Black – enforcer of Rangers and Hearts teams of the 80s. Encounters with Kenny were fairly brutal, but I never backed down. The 1986 Scottish Cup quarter final at Tynecastle basically ended up in an on-pitch battle, driven on by Kenny and myself.

7. Walter Kidd – Black's Hearts team-mate. Looked like Skeletor – with less charm. Many a winger disappeared when up against Kidd, as if he were The Gorgie's equivalent of the Bermuda Triangle.

6. Neil Simpson – quiet, effective and ruthless. Simpson was the bouncer who looked after the midfield of the outstanding Aberdeen team of the 80s and was a feared opponent. Unfortunately for Simpson, he overstepped the mark in October 1988 with a well-documented stamp on Ian Durrant's knee. By all accounts this was completely out of character for Simpson, but he was hounded out of Scottish football and played out his career in the English lower leagues.

5. Willie Miller – widely recognised as a world class sweeper - and referee. Willie could take you out without anyone - including the victim - being aware that anything untoward had taken place. If he was seen by the officials, no action was taken, as Willie was the fourth official before they invented a fourth official. Ahead of his time in so many ways was Willie.

4. Cammy Fraser – in the early 80s, Rangers were in the doldrums. Ibrox was no longer a place to fear going to – it was just another league match and we expected to get something out of the games. Cammy was employed as Rangers' muscle in midfield, but not to the entire approval of the Ibrox hordes. In fact he caused quite a stir when he publicly V-signed the Govan Stand while playing for Rangers. In a league game, at Ibrox, we both went for a 50/50. Cammy went low, I went high. As Cammy went for the double leg amputation just above the ankle, my own full-length lunge meant that I cleared his entire body like a hurdler. The ball was untouched by either of us. The ref stood open jawed and no cards were even brought out, let alone a foul given - no contact was made so wild were the challenges. Bizarrely, I found that half the Rangers fans were applauding me and urging me to go and finish him off. With friends like that…

3. Graeme Souness – world-class midfielder and borderline psychopath on the pitch. Most were intimidated by his presence, but I couldn't wait to have a go with him. In season 1986-87, his first season at Rangers, we came up against each other at Love Street – Souness limped off, substituting himself. 'I'll f*****g see you at Ibrox, Abercromby' were his parting words. There was more to that threat than met the eye, as will be documented later, but nobody came close to having that permanent air of menace that Souness had. You always felt the clock was ticking.

2. Jimmy Case – Souness' midfield partner at Liverpool and a genuinely legendary hard man. We played against each other in 1977, but without much incident. Ten years later we met again, in Singapore when Jimmy was playing for Southampton. The tackles were flying in and you could tell that we were set on collision course – it was just a matter of when. A ball broke loose and slowly rolled ten yards from each of us. Geronimo! This was a speciality tackle for both of us – masters of the art. BANG ! The ball didn't move. We just looked at each other, smiled then laughed. We had met each other's match and we were both still standing.

1. John 'Cowboy' McCormack – not an opponent, but a team-mate. I'll put it simply: John had no pain threshold. He once played an entire 90 minutes with a broken toe – and no painkillers. Ricky McFarlane was astonished, being a physio by trade and mumbled words like 'it's just not right… impossible'. If someone got past me, then their 'reward' was usually an encounter with 'The Cowboy'. And that was usually the end of that.

Missing from the Top 10 is legendary Motherwell and Rangers full-back Gregor Stevens. Gregor is disqualified on the grounds that being a walking lunatic on the field of play does not count.

Of course, it goes without saying that if all of the above had been playing in the modern era, then most, including myself, would probably have spent half the season suspended - apart from Willie Miller for the refereeing reason already stated. Protecting the skill players is admirable, but the removal of contact from the game today is something that has probably gone too far – especially in comparison to the comparative lack of punishment issued to other less admirable traits of professional football, particularly simulation or diving.

I do have a wee chortle when I see the likes of Derek Johnstone and Gordon Smith bemoaning the way that 'foreigners have brought diving to our game'. Jesus – these guys obviously have a memory block. Derek 'DJ' Johnstone once got Doug Rougvie sent off in a Cup Final, simply by falling over and clutching his big coupon after Doug ventured to within two feet of him – no contact was made whatsoever and it is as embarrassing to watch today as it was back in the 70s. Big DJ" and Smith were Rangers team-mates of John 'Polaris' McDonald, a striker who seemed to be permanently pre-programmed to dive – particularly within opponents' penalty boxes. Everybody knew what was going on, but for some reason 'Polaris' was rarely caught by the refs and this was before diving was even a yellow card offence. Every team had at least one player who went down easily if required including St Mirren, although I'm not going to mention who our penalty-winner was! So, I can assure younger readers that diving is not a modern phenomenon. Fortunately, I rarely had a direct problem with divers – most of the refs were left in no uncertainty if I had done the likes of 'Polaris'.

The game is much faster now, but probably the poorer for it. Players are stronger, faster and fitter. Consequently, simple athleticism is a valued commodity and players can easily be deployed in numbers to stop teams playing, but offering very little in the way of entertainment themselves.

I played in an era when the flair players had more time to express themselves and the defenders had more leeway to combat this with barely legal brutality. There were skills to be learnt on both counts and supporters were arguably treated to more entertainment in the form of good versus evil confrontations taking place on a weekly basis. The absence of blanket

ABER'S GONNAE GET YE!

TV coverage, multi-angle cameras and TV evidence being used by the football authorities were also crucial for the above ten players, plus myself, being able to survive and prosper within the game.

One thing that is rarely covered is the fact that players were often an on-pitch police force and a lot of nonsense carried out by players, that was missed by the referee, would always be righted through off the ball incidents. I regularly had run-ins with opponents who had been taking serious liberties with us, for example either through diving to try and con the ref, or making sneaky challenges to try and intimidate younger players.

Perpetrators would be punched or whacked when the referee's back was turned or their attention was focused elsewhere. Goalkeeper clearances were always a good time to act quickly and the ironic thing is that more often than not, the opposition team knew what had gone on and if a player deserved it and they knew that the ref hadn't seen it, then few complaints were raised. That was the law of the jungle and some of us were better geared for survival than others.

4 The Saints Go Marching In

IN 1978-79, we aimed to cement our position in the league and try and push into the top four of the table. As was becoming our new-found tradition, we entered the Anglo-Scottish Cup with great enthusiasm. We were paired up with Bristol City in the quarter-final and some revenge was to be had. Rikki Sharpe (brother of Everton star Graeme) scored both goals as we beat Bristol 2-0 at Love Street in the first leg and in the return game, I scored in a 2—2 draw that saw us through to the semis. Unfortunately, back-to-back 1-1 draws, with Billy Stark scoring for Saints in each tie, saw Oldham Athletic defeat us 4-2 on penalties at Love Street.

Our ambitions for league position improvement got off to a great start with an opening day 1-0 win against Rangers at Ibrox, with Bobby Torrance scoring a late winner. A couple of weeks later we won the local derby down at Greenock, beating Morton 3-1, with yours truly scoring the third to kill the game with ten minutes to go.

Over the next couple of months we were reasonably solid, with the new version of the team not really gelling until later in the year. Then we really got going. A Frank McGarvey goal saw us beat Motherwell 1-0 and go joint top of the Premier League with Rangers in February – only 18 months after the club played its first ever Premier League game.

A stormy 2-2 draw at Love Street with Aberdeen a week later saw us go clear at the top. Goals from Steve Archibald and Gordon Strachan saw us 2-0 down with about 20 minutes to go, before all Hell let loose, much to Fergie's volcanic-like fury in the visitor's dug-out. Dons' captain, Willie Miller and my future team-mate, Ian Scanlon were sent off, sandwiched by goals from Frank McGarvey and Jackie Copland.

After the game, it transpired that Fergie's Dad had died in hospital just up the road at the same time the mayhem was being unleashed. Alex was also in the middle of his unsuccessful tribunal against St Mirren over his sacking and a few of our players felt for him once we heard the news.

By this time McGarvey was on fire - an image that many Rangers and Morton fans would enjoy if that was literally the case - scoring five goals in two games as Partick Thistle and Morton were collectively gubbed out of sight. There was not much of the season left and the finishing line was in sight. Could the impossible dream be realised? Could St Mirren win the Premier League? Sadly, it all went wrong very quickly.

We lost three games at Love Street on the bounce in a disastrous run of six defeats in seven games, often losing by a single goal. Further defeats to Celtic and Morton further added to the woes.

Due to a severe winter in Scotland that year there was a fixture pile-up and we actually played Celtic three times in the run-in - and lost the lot, including a 'home game' for Saints that was played at Ibrox, as Love Street had started to be redeveloped before the season ended. Did the planners know something we didn't?

A great win against Fergie's Aberdeen boys at Pittodrie couldn't mask the disappointment as we slid down the table and finished in sixth place. Had we bottled it? I don't know – you'd need to ask all the players for their own honest views, but I think that we simply panicked. Actually, that might be a bit unfair, as the combination of inexperience with tiredness during the fixture-packed end of season run-in was what probably did for us.

One thing was for sure, it did give us a lesson on the levels of consistency required to keep pushing up the league and it was a lesson that would serve this squad of players very, very well in the coming seasons.

St Mirren would only finish outside of the top five once in the next six seasons – a magnificent achievement, given the size of the club in comparison to the neighbouring Glasgow giants and the then all-powerful forces of Aberdeen and Dundee United, who were cutting a swathe through Europe at the same time.

It was the 1979-1980 season that was momentous for all at Love Street and probably ranks as one of the most successful years in the club's history. The team was now functioning as a well-drilled unit and confidence was high, with the new frontline of Bone, Somner and MacDougall providing a serious threat to all opposition. Unfortunately, I missed a small chunk of it in mid-season following a training injury.

Due to bad weather, we were training indoors at Barrhead High School and during a five-a-side game I was just about to shoot, when Lex Richardson felled me with a mistimed challenge. I knew something was badly wrong with my leg and I went white as a sheet. Big Jim Clunie said: 'There's bugger all wrong with you son - I'll see you tomorrow.' I went home and soon was in utter agony. I phoned for an ambulance and was taken to the Royal Alexandra Infirmary. Before the ambulance came I phoned the boss and told him what I was doing.

'Alright Aber, if you don't make training tomorrow, I'll pop up to the hospital and see how you're doing'. He was all heart, was Jim! When he arrived at the RAI, Clunie tracked me down and was met with the sight of his player sitting in bed with a plaster cast on his leg - I had broken it. Cheers Lex. Luckily, I was a quick-healer and was out of action for only a couple of months or so and was able to get back in the team just in time for the Anglo-Scottish Cup Final.

That season's Anglo-Scottish Cup campaign was hugely successful. The early round saw us despatch Hibs 4-0 on aggregate, before a tumultuous quarter-final tie with Bolton Wanderers. The first leg in Paisley saw us run out convincing 4-2 winners, with Stark, McDougall (2) and Bone being the Saints scorers, against a strong Bolton team, featuring the likes of Frank Worthington and Sam Allardyce.

The first half was one of the finest performances seen by a St Mirren side in decades, with us being 4-0 up at one point before half-time. Down in Lancashire, we thought we were out, as with 90 minutes up we trailed 2-0 at Burnden Park. Jimmy Bone had other ideas and in an injury time breakaway, he scored a cracker with the last kick of the ball to send us into the semis.

Next up was Sheffield United and after a creditable 0-0 draw at Bramall Lane, the Saints beat the Blades 4-0 at Love Street, with Billy Stark - again - Iain Munro and Doug Somner (2) doing the damage. Who else were we to play in the final, but Bristol City?

In the first leg, we went to Bristol, firmly with the intention of gaining revenge on the final loss two years previously. There was a familiar face in the opposition line-up – Fitzy. Tony was in the middle of his spell at Ashton Gate and this final must have been a dream/nightmare tie for him. Tony only played in the first leg, missing the return at Love Street due to injury, but suffered even more as we ran out 2-0 winners, with Billy Stark - he must have loved this tournament - scoring both goals.

A couple of weeks later, on 16th April 1980, the second leg was played at Love Street. Alex Beckett was injured and his misfortune was my good luck, as I had just returned from my broken leg and played in a couple of reserve matches. Clunie selected me and this was the biggest night of my career so far. Love Street was packed and the highlights were to be televised later that night on BBC1. In the pre-Sky days, this was a big deal.

A couple of goals from Doug Somner and a strike from wee Alan Logan saw Saints go 3-0 up on the night and although Bristol City pulled one back, the 5-1 aggregate victory was a great achievement.

St Mirren was the first and only Scottish team to win the trophy and the celebrations went long into the night in the Paisley area. We were all bursting with pride and I think the fans felt the same as well.

This is one of the fantastic things about playing for a provincial club – when success IS achieved, the feeling of the players and the fans being in it together is tangible. It's arguably more enjoyable than success achieved at major clubs, where such success is expected – at least that's what Frank McGarvey says and he should know.

Brian Clough went on record as saying that Nottingham Forest's success in the Anglo-Scottish Cup a few years earlier was instrumental in turning around the fortunes of Nottingham Forest. By strange coincidence, Forest retained the European Cup a few weeks after our triumph against Bristol City, beating Hamburg 1-0 in the Bernabau. The dreamers of the St Mirren faithful could have good reason to think 'what if?' when this point is considered.

The 1979-1980 league campaign started appallingly, maybe as a hangover from the disappointment of the previous season's run-in and also as new signings were finding their feet in the team. Saying that, we were absolutely garbage for the first few weeks of the season and looked like nailed-on certainties for relegation.

Big Jim might have been worried, but he never let the players know. He did, of course point out our scary shortcomings in those opening weeks, in his own inimitable direct style, which was to be his undoing at Love Street – but more of that later.

Games against Kilmarnock, Dundee, Morton and Rangers saw us amass only one single point. The bad run carried on right through until the end of October. I believe that the Anglo-Scottish Cup run at the same period was proving a welcome distraction from the worries about the league form.

ABER'S GONNAE GET YE!

Sheffield and Bolton may not be everyone's idea of escapist retreats, but free from the worries of our dire league form, we played some great football and it helped bring back some confidence in the squad that had been beginning to erode alarmingly.

We were going down faster than a knackered lift in the eyes of the press, some of whom had got a bit hacked off - bad pun, I know - at these upstarts from Paisley gaining praise for their attacking football and upsetting the odds on more than a few occasions. Their private joy was to be short-lived, as the return of the Saints was just around the corner as we came storming back in some style.

A 4-2 win over Dundee, at Love Street on the last Saturday of October was the catalyst that we had been waiting for. Shortly afterwards, Rangers were beaten 2-1 in Paisley and we were up and running, albeit three months late.

Hibs were the next victims of a 2-1 defeat in Paisley, but that game was remembered more for the Scottish League debut of Hibs left-winger, George Best. A massive crowd piled in to Love Street to see Bestie make his Hibs debut and he did conjure up some magic for the fans – but happily not at our expense.

George was largely anonymous for the entire game - to be fair, he wasn't exactly at the peak of his powers then, but when Doug Somner put us 2-0 up with two minutes to go, it was as if George realised he should really start playing now. He immediately scored a superb solo effort, making it 2-1 with time almost up. In injury time, he went on another mazy run and almost equalised. As far as cameo appearances go, it was fairly spectacular.

After the game, George came into the players' lounge and like something out of an old western, silence descended. He had recently had antabuse pellets sewn into his stomach to try and combat his alcoholism and everyone in the room was staring at George as he went up to the bar. 'Orange juice please,' he says as the famous Irish accent shattered the silence. George turned round to flash that big smile to all of us in the room and the place erupted in laughter. You could say that he took it in good spirit – and if anyone is allowed to make a joke like that, then I am that man.

Celtic were then beaten 2-1 at Love Street and Doug Somner was now recognised as the most dangerous striker in Scotland. From the gloom of a couple of months earlier, we were now riding high and feared no one.

Rangers were beaten 2-1 at Ibrox, with Doug scoring a last minute winner, before Dundee United were beaten 2-1 again being the result, with Doug scoring both.

On the run continued and in March we went to Parkhead to play Celtic. With less than eight weeks to go, the title was set to be won by either Aberdeen, Celtic, or St Mirren. This was a big game. With 20 minutes to go, we were 2-0 down, but up popped Mr. Somner with a quick brace and we managed a 2-2 draw. This time we thought that we were in with a real chance of making history.

Unfortunately, we lost a local derby against Morton in Greenock and it was to be an important result. Jimmy Bone put us ahead and it was all systems go, but as is always the way in derby matches, form meant nothing. The great Andy Ritchie equalised for The Ton, before John Young scored an unfortunate own goal to seal the game for Morton.

We battered them for the last 30 minutes, but to no avail. Unlike the previous season, we didn't go into some kind of tailspin and kept plugging away, but it was a valuable two points dropped – never mind the local bragging rights. St Mirren were aiming higher than that. The Anglo-Scottish Cup Final victory boosted morale and combined with the memories of the previous year, we were determined to give it a real go in the final games.

Aberdeen were being remorseless as Fergie went after his first Premier League title and seemed to be winning every week. We were doing OK, but would occasionally drop a point in drawn matches that we should have won. This is where titles are won and lost and the old cliché about grinding out results is completely true. Nonetheless, with only three games left we were still in with a good shout of the title when we made the trip to Aberdeen on 26th April.

Win and it was game on for the title. Lose and we would be almost certainly out of it. Fergie had his team well fired-up, as you could imagine with all the recent history between him and St Mirren, factored in with his obsessive desire to get that first title.

Aberdeen blitzed us in the first half and we were 2-0 down at half-time, with goals from Ian Scanlon and my old adversary Doug Rougvie. The second half was a different matter, but as much as we bombarded the home goal, nothing constructive came of our efforts and the emerging Miller and McLeish partnership stood firm. The disappointment amongst the players was massive, but not as much as the Paisley fans who had travelled North in great numbers. Soon afterwards we lost 2-1 to Hibs in Edinburgh, despite taking an early lead and this effectively finished our title aspirations.

However, we were to go out with a bang and the final game of the season was at Love Street against Rangers. Jimmy Bone and a Doug Somner hat-trick saw us finish in some style with a 4-1 trouncing of the 'Gers in front of our own fans. It was a great day and saw St Mirren achieve their highest league position for almost 90 years – a proud fact that remains to this day. This is something that I am immensely proud of, as are the rest of the players of that squad and there is still a bond between us that has stood the test of time as well.

PREMIER DIVISION FINAL TABLE 1979/80

	PLD	W	D	L	F	A	PTS	
1. Aberdeen	36	19	10	7	68	36	48	*Champions*
2. Celtic	36	18	11	7	61	38	47	
3. St Mirren	36	15	12	9	56	49	42	
4. Dundee United	36	12	13	11	43	30	37	
5. Rangers	36	15	7	14	50	46	37	
6. Morton	36	14	8	14	51	46	36	
7. Partick Thistle	36	11	14	11	43	47	36	
8. Kilmarnock	36	11	11	14	36	52	33	
9. Dundee	36	10	6	20	47	73	26	*Relegated*
10. Hibernian	36	6	6	24	29	67	18	*Relegated*

Around this time, Love Street was scene to some truly bizarre pre-match and half-time entertainment, as the club tried to inject a bit of razzle-dazzle into match days in Paisley, taking inspiration from Americans. As we warmed up before games, players and fans were treated, if that is the right word, to routines from a troupe of majorettes. Bonnie Barr's Majorettes they were called and these poor wee lassies would dance around the outskirts of the pitch, invariably in freezing conditions, doing some strange kind of cheerleading routine for the benefit of a startled looking Paisley public, some of whom would make dubious remarks to the girls, which really wasn't helping matters.

The players? We just got on with our usual warm-up, but there was a fair bit of amusement when the troupe first appeared. I think you can imagine some of the comments that flew around the dressing room of a professional football team. This was definitely not what happened in the

North American Soccer League– it was more Cosmo Chippy – a Love Street eaterie for those who have never sampled its deep-fried delights - than New York Cosmos.

However, the genuine article did appear when Saints played a friendly against Tampa Bay Rowdies. Sadly, this was in Paisley and not Florida, but the Rowdies brought a fair smattering of stars with them, including famous playboy, full-time pundit and occasional player, the great Rodney Marsh.

On a personal note, I achieved one my life's ambitions when I was called up for the Scotland Under-21 squad to play in Portugal. Eddie Turnbull was the Under-21 manager, with Ricky McFarlane being his assistant. What was even more encouraging was that is widely known that Jock Stein was having a heavy influence on the Under-21 set-up from his position as national team manager. If Big Jock thought that I was worth a call-up then I really must have been doing something right.

Eddie was a bit of a disciplinarian, possibly to an eccentric level, but then again, he was in charge of a group of daft young footballers from Scotland and trying to keep us disciplined as we travelled about Europe was enough to test any man.

He used to go crazy in particular if you had your hands in your tracksuit bottoms. On one occasion, I was standing on the training ground, talking to Ricky McFarlane and Eddie bellowed: 'You two! Get your hands out of your pockets - NOW!' Ricky – Eddie's assistant – could barely conceal his laughter at being the latest victim of Eddie's obsession.

Looking back on the squad of players in that Under-21 team, it really was a terrific group: Billy Thomson, Roy Aitken, Bobby Russell, Murdo McLeod, Eamonn Bannon, John Wark and last, but not least, my room-mate Alan Brazil.

'Baz' was a great guy, with a infectious love of life and a wicked sense of humour. Everything seemed to be a joke for him and it was no surprise to see him develop a great career at the pinnacle of the English game with Ipswich Town. He was unflappable and the only nerves he showed were usually in relation to the racing results. Alan's hairstyle was the blonde complement to the Afros of Roy Aitken and myself and we looked like the Hair Bear Bunch, or as someone cruelly put it, The Temptations…if they had only come from Glasgow.

I finally made my International debut in an away tie in Norway. I was put on with about 30 minutes to go and we were trailing 1-0. With just a couple of minutes left, I played a one-two with Jim Melrose on the left flank, which saw me through one-on-one with the keeper. I curled it past him, but the ball smacked off the post into the goalmouth and was cleared by a defender.

Ricky said to me after the game that if it had gone in, then my name would have been all over the papers and I would have attracted the attention of some bigger teams. Something that may not have benefited him in his role at Love Street) but it wasn't to be. I made seven squads for the Under-21s and was extremely proud to have done so. I just wish it had been more.

Prior to the start of the 1980-81 season, I got my first taste of playing a final at Hampden Park. The Drybrough Cup was a short, pre-season tournament and we qualified as one of the top eight goal-scoring teams from the previous season. The format was simple: quarter final when we beat Falkirk 2-0; semi-final when we beat Ayr United 2-1, then a Final at Hampden. On this occasion, we played Aberdeen in the Final and whilst it was basically a pre-season workout, it was still a final at Hampden. Alas, we lost 2-1, but I would be back in seven years time for a proper final.

However, something else had been achieved from our great season. St Mirren had qualified for the UEFA Cup because of our third place finishing position in the league. History had been made and Paisley was to be represented in Europe by something more than a W.H. Malcolm freight lorry at Calais docks.

The standards that we had now set were to be the blueprint for a period of success at St Mirren that had never been seen in Paisley for decades and has not been repeated since – although I would be as happy as any Buddie to see the good time come back to St Mirren. Although I was born in Paisley, my childhood was in Glasgow and I would be lying if I said that I was a St Mirren fan as a boy. However, my 13-year association with the club has been one of the most dominant features of my life and I firmly regard St Mirren as my team.

Between 1978 and 1987 St Mirren finished every season in the top seven of the Scottish Premier League, including five top five finishes; we qualified for European football four times; and won the club's first major trophy for almost 30 years. We were in the midst of a golden era for St Mirren and to be honest, it all became a bit of a blur as the rollercoaster ride kept picking up speed.

ABER'S GONNAE GET YE!

The games came thick and fast and we relentlessly met the challenge each and every year, continually confounding the Press's scepticism for our chances and punching way above our weight on a regular basis. With the Scottish Premier League having a format of 10 teams playing each other four times a year, plus factoring in cup games, there was certainly a case of familiarity breeding contempt amongst most of the teams. There were a lot of very, very good players in the SPL during this era. Of the players that I played directly against on the pitch, there were about half a dozen that really stand out when looking back at the era.

Celtic's Paul McStay was a nightmare for me to play against. He had it all. Good with both feet, not afraid to tackle, great passing vision, a knack of scoring vital goals and an engine that was second to none. Paul was always on the move – it was impossible to man-mark him and there was no way I was going to run around after him all day long.

Towards the end of my career, I came up against Rangers' very own version of McStay, in the shape of Ian Durrant. Tons of skill and a knack of direct forward running with the ball, while also picking out passes with ease, he was a real talent. Unfortunately, his career was never quite the same following the aforementioned incident with Aberdeen's Neil Simpson, in 1988. Durranty was one of the good guys and could respect what opponents like myself were all about – he seemed to relish the challenge.

Up at Aberdeen, Fergie had resurrected the career of a diminutive midfielder by the name of Gordon Strachan. I would have preferred it if my old boss had not carried out this piece of talent-finding. Strachan was a busy wee player – over-flowing with skill, matched only by his chronic case of wee man syndrome. He was always nipping away at you, be it verbals, or snidey challenges, often off the ball. To be fair, Gordon probably had to master these arts to look after himself on the mean fields of Scottish football, but when combined with his massive ability, he was one serious pain in the arse of an opponent.

He was a magnet for abuse from all opposition fans, culminating in a Celtic fan running out of The Jungle at Parkhead and planting one on the wee man. Something many of his opponents had only dreamed of doing. We had several run-ins over the years and even now, long after we have retired, my pulse quickens when I see him on TV being interviewed. Aber's Gonnae Get Ye! Yes, one day, Gordon… probably when we're both 80 odd.

Tommy Burns was also a very, very difficult opponent. Comfortable on the ball, he never seemed to stop running and to put it plainly, in the last 20 minutes of games, it was tough keeping up with him. I was fit, no question, but Burns seemed to be on a different level to all the players on the rest of the park. This probably goes some way to explain the number of late goals that he was involved in for Celtic. Tommy had a bit of a temper though and this was one area that you worked him on - if you were prepared to risk the ginger volcanic eruption.

One player who never got the recognition he deserved was Bobby Russell of Rangers and Motherwell. Bobby had a fabulous first touch and a great footballing brain, which helped him make a fool of many an opponent, including my good self. In the early 80s, Rangers went into a downward spiral and I sometimes wonder what recognition Bobby would have got had he been playing with better team-mates.

One team-mate of Bobby's who certainly was good enough was Jim Bett and who also went on to have a great career at Aberdeen. He was signed by Fergie – who else? Jim was a big fella and it was impossible to get the ball off him without committing a foul. He combined his physical strength with a sublime amount of skill, but somehow never appeared to be in a hurry, or particularly flustered.

This apparent air of casualness counted against him in the eyes of the Press, with allegations of laziness doing the rounds. I can assure you that Jim Bett was not lazy. Don't take my word for it – the mere fact that the late great Jock Stein repeatedly picked him to play in a Scotland midfield with the likes of Souness and Dalglish should be enough to dispel those thoughts.

One thing all those guys had in common was they were all workers – a characteristic admired by both team-mates and opponents and more so than today, you had to fight the battle first to earn the right to play. I guess this is where I came into the equation in the eyes of the various managers I played for at St Mirren. As my pal Fitzy would put it: 'Hard work only beats talent, when talent doesn't work hard enough'. I think my efforts were appreciated by my team-mates – none were shirkers on the physical side of things, but going toe-to-toe with the likes of Kenny Black was certainly an acquired taste – but one which I seemed to have a natural appetite for.

ABER'S GONNAE GET YE!

5 Over Land And Sea

AS the team's domestic success progressed so did the places we were playing at. The Anglo-Scottish Cup runs had seen us visiting some of the less fashionable, but successful, English clubs and of course we did get to play Liverpool in 1977. I had always liked to travel, going back to my wee sojourn in Great Yarmouth and my horizons were about to be broadened as we embarked on another set of new experiences.

This was the continuing evolution of a great wee club and the experiences were as new to the fans as they were to the players – it was a magical time. Throughout this period, players left and new faces came in, but the spirit and camaraderie remained intact – arguably growing even stronger. Also, our impending travels were also to be the setting for yet more managerial upheaval and one of the most shattering defeats that we had ever experienced.

It all started so well, with an amazing trip to Brazil in the close season of 1980. Passports were now required for the away games and in some cases this actually was the case, as some players had to get passports to travel for this tour. You've never seen as many people run so quickly to the passport office. Rio de Janeiro - I don't know who organised this tour, it was possibly one of the Directors who was involved in the whisky trade, but I would like to take this opportunity to thank him for what was probably the best jolly I have ever been on.

On arrival to our swanky Five Star hotel in Rio, we couldn't help but notice the banks of limos outside, complete with blacked out windows. Not for a minute did we think that they were for our use and soon after we checked into the rooms, it was time for some exploring.

Lex Richardson was my room-mate as normal and we walked past the limos and hired a local rickshaw carrier. We immediately tipped him the local equivalent of six months wages, about £10 and from that moment on he couldn't have been more obliging. Through the streets of Rio we went, Julio Iglesias blasting out of the lad's ghetto blaster that was nestled between Lexy and myself. It was the time of the local carnival and we had eyes out on stalks at some of the sights we saw – it was a long, long way from Possil and Barrhead that's for sure.

As our very rough guide to Rio continued clattering along the streets, a big black Mercedes limo with the blacked out windows drew level. The rear window slid down and out popped the head of one of the directors, John Corson, looking stunned at finding two of his star players being ferried round Rio on a rickshaw. 'You can use the hotel cars, ya pair of dafties,' was his cry, just in time for the Merc to glide off up the road. It didn't seem half as much fun, though.

In and around some training sessions and the odd friendly against some local lower-league outfits, the team-bonding/tourism trip continued apace. Next up was a visit to the Maracana to see the Brazilian Cup Final. The legendary Zico was playing for one of the sides, Flamenco, but to be honest we weren't taking too much notice of the match action.

The place was a lunatic asylum, with a crowd of 175,000, large chunks of whom spent the entire 90 minutes having a battle with each other. The whole St Mirren party were sh******g themselves. It had taken about two hours to get from the surroundings of the ground to our seats and we had been told to expect almost four hours to get out.

What better time than this for club director, John Corson to start a row with the locals. Somebody kept standing up obscuring John's view of the game and he took serious umbrage at this, standing up and gesticulating at the guy in question to sit down. Next thing you know, our party were getting all manner of evil stares, threats and throat-slitting gestures. And we weren't even in Greenock.

The appropriately named Sunset Club, which appeared to have a 24-hour licence, was near to our hotel. Around 4am, the phone rang in our room. It was big Doug Somner.

'Are ye thirsty Aber?' was his question.

From that point on, the social side of the trip started to get a bit silly, with night and day blending into one gigantic bevvy session in the neon wonderland of the Sunset Club. My highlight was a prototype karaoke evening – and this was years before this singing activity was popular in Scotland. We were knocking back the Pink Ladies – and drinking some cocktails as well. Various tunes were being played over the PA and there was a microphone on hand if you fancied your chances at joining in.

All the usual suspects had a go. Papa Bone, Lexy, John Young - who was a good singer if I remember rightly - Big Frank and The Drambuie Kid himself, Alex Beckett, whose rabid renditions were in a strange hybrid of Scots and Brazilian. The place was in uproar and we were even getting requests from fellow drinkers.

In the meantime, we were spiking Ricky's cocktails and he was soon mildly plastered. Buddy Holly came over the PA. 'Hey - I want a go," a shout came from the throng. It was Ricky. We were initially stunned, then shortly afterwards nearly p*****g ourselves laughing as our assistant manager was holding court to the entire place, regaling them with his unique takes on That'll Be The Day and Peggy Sue. I think Ricky enjoyed it, because once the king-size hangover disappeared, he saw the funny side. As did Jim Clunie, who spent most of his spare time enjoying the sunshine and cocktails with a permanently fixed grin on his face. It was a brilliant trip for all concerned. I think the locals enjoyed our visit as well – at least the ladies did.

On the flight back to Heathrow, most of the players and staff were sleeping. It was a scheduled flight and we were all seated in a fairly large group, spread over three or four rows of the 747. We were fairly noticeable as a football team on tour, but the initial noise and excitement at flying home to tell our not- so-tall tales from the exotic backdrop of Rio de Janeiro soon disappeared as we all began to nod off. We were knackered – and it was hardly surprising.

As a meal was about to be served and most of us were waking up from dreams about girls on Copacabana beach, sorry, scoring the winner at the Maracana, I noticed that our long-time kit man, Jackie Gough appeared to be still out for the count.

Jackie was sitting beside me, so I nudged him and said: 'C'mon Jackie, wakey, wakey - the meal's coming round.'

Nothing.

'C'mon Jackie, waken up.'

Still nothing.

'Jackie…..Jackie!'

A horrible thought cut through my head, clearing any residue of an alcoholic haze that had been topped up with the drinks on the flight home. I noticed that Jackie was still and his skin chalk white. And when I touched him to shake him from his slumbers, he felt strangely cold.

'Jesus Christ…..he's dead', I thought.

I quietly muttered 'Oh shit' to myself and sought out the slumbering figure of Ricky McFarlane who was sitting close by. I left my aisle seat and shook Ricky awake.

'Ricky – there's something seriously wrong with Jackie – you'd better come and have a look,' I said anxiously.

Ricky seemed like the logical choice to get help from, as he had a good medical knowledge and was one of the few sane heads in that group.

An ashen-faced Ricky quickly confirmed the news I had feared that Jackie had, in fact, passed away sitting beside me on that plane.

I had never seen a dead body before, let alone someone who I knew so well and was friendly with. I was utterly stunned – my feet seemed glued to the spot and although I could see that Ricky was talking to me, I just wasn't taking anything in. It was as if I had cotton wool in my ears and everything seemed to be going in slow-motion.

The murmurs grew quickly as the rest of the Saints party were made aware of what had happened and some of the senior pros who had known Jackie for a long time came over to see what was going on.

It must have been obvious to anyone else on the plane that something had gone badly wrong and the murmurs grew louder. Ricky had called in the cabin crew and very soon we cleared the middle row, where Jackie was laid out, while Ricky and the crew took charge of the situation. The stewardesses, still professional, but obviously upset, used the privacy curtains to erect a screen around Jackie and soon the Tannoy cracked into life telling passengers that the plane was diverting to Frankfurt. This was apparently standard aviation practice, and we were to go to the first major airport that would take us, so that the events could be quickly investigated. This is where Jackie was to be taken from the plane and his body driven to a mortuary, before being flown home to Paisley.

This all happened before the age of mobile phones and when we landed in Germany, Big Jim Clunie and Ricky McFarlane tried to get hold of Jackie's wife back in Paisley, but to no avail. By the time we had been re-routed and touched down at Glasgow Airport, a couple of miles from the

Gough's house, in Paisley, poor Mrs.Gough had already found out about her husband's death from the news bulletin on local radio.

I cannot even start to imagine what she must have been feeling. Jackie was a smashing wee guy and loved by everyone at Love Street and this was devastating for all of us. A post-mortem later confirmed that he had died in his sleep of a heart attack, but these were the days before deep vein thrombosis was talked about and I sometimes wonder if the long-haul flight was what did for him.

Only days after our Karaoke experience, Big Jim and Ricky were having to field questions from the waiting media about the tragic events. The whole episode was tortuous and none of us who were there will ever forget it. RIP Jackie.

As mentioned earlier, the great 1980 season saw us qualify for the UEFA Cup. It is fair to say that we entered the tournament as innocents abroad, without a shred of European experience among us. The draw had given us a first round tie against IF Elfsborg, from Sweden. Not exactly a household European name, but that was soon to be rectified.

St Mirren's first ever European tie was played in the Ryavallen Stadium, on 17th September 1980. The team had been augmented by the summer signing of John 'Cowboy' McCormack, from Clydebank. I think it is fair to say that 'Cowboy' was a competitive player and although initially played at right-back, John also spent a lot of time in a defensive midfield position. The combination of the two of us certainly was an explosive combination for any opposition teams to tackle - in every sense of the word.

'Cowboy' was a winner and would put 110 per cent effort into trying to win at whatever challenge was put his way. He was a great guy off the pitch, although there were moments when his fiery competitiveness brought him into direct opposition with myself, even as a team-mate.

One day, while getting ready at Love Street to go training at nearby Abbotsinch, John and I had a wee verbal spat. Nothing new there, but this one seemed to escalate – I cannot even remember what it was actually all about and I would be surprised if John could either.

However, the boxing gloves were almost on in the changing room, only for us to be saved by the bell, as the call came that the bus was ready to take us training. This was a temporary ceasefire. 'I'll see you out there Aber', was John's message as we filed out of the boot room. The pin had been pulled.

A practice match began, with us put in separate teams - not a wise move

- and a loose ball presented the perfect 50/50 for both of us. Both of us thought f**k the ball and we launched into ridiculously over the top tackles, quickly followed by the inevitable explosive punch-up. Ricky and other players came piling in to try and separate us and calm was eventually restored.

I will claim to be the victor in that spat, simply because Ricky said that he had fined John and not me as John was being louder than me - I preferred the quiet assassin role and any bystanders would have seen him as the blatant aggressor.

John was always very vocal and animated - with anyone within a mile getting a clear commentary of his grievances and what he was going to do to me. I had more of a quiet way regarding delivering my menace. As a consequence, the whole incident was viewed as John being aggressive towards me, and I was just defending myself. It was one of the few occasions when I escaped the clutches of St Mirren's internal disciplinary measures during my career.

As for the combatants, well we had forgotten about it all by that afternoon – the air had been well and truly cleared. God knows what anyone driving past the pitches at Abbotsinch that morning would have thought.

In the first leg in Sweden, we got off to a terrible start and were lucky to be only 1-0 down when Doug Somner scored a cracker right on half-time. Boosted by this, we dominated the second half and it was well deserved when 'Starsky' cut a ball back for me to smash home for the winner with about 20 minutes to go. As I said, I didn't score many goals, but when they did go in, they were often very important and scoring the winner in St Mirren's first-ever European tie is something I am very proud of.

A couple of weeks later saw Love Street's first ever European night, but unfortunately it was a bit of a let-down, with a scrappy 0-0 draw being the outcome. Nonetheless, the Saints went marching in to the second-round draw. This was where we realised our dream of getting a shot at one of Europe's famous big guns. French giants, St Etienne were our opposition and what a set of players they had: Michel Platini, Patrick Battiston, Jacques Santini and Johnny Rep were in their squad – this really was going to be a severe test against some of the elite of European talent.

On 22nd October 1980, St Mirren played St Etienne, in what a few years previously would have been thought as the most unlikely battle of the Saints. A good crowd of about 12,000 was there and the atmosphere was

ABER'S GONNAE GET YE!

fantastic – despite the standard Paisley monsoon. We played very, very well and by the second half we were in complete control against one of Europe's top sides. Unfortunately, to get that status, the French team knew exactly how to handle these situations and no matter how much pressure we exerted, their defence stood firm, happy with the 0-0 result.

The return leg was played on 5th November, Guy Fawkes night back at home, but there was to be no shortages of fireworks on this trip, as the next few days were to be fairly dramatic. Nobody gave us much of a chance, but St Etienne had not scored in Paisley and this gave us the huge incentive of trying to nick a breakaway goal because of the away-goals-count-double rule that would see us to the next round should we manage to force a draw.

Unfortunately, the quality of St Etienne showed through in the return leg, as they ran out 2-0 winners. Still, we played very well and gave a great account of ourselves over the two ties, but they were simply the best team that we had played against in a competitive match.

Apart from the luminaries mentioned earlier, I felt the real star of the show was a big fella called Larios. Of Algerian descent, he reminded me of the Big Chief in the One Flew Over The Cuckoos Nest movie and he simply dominated the whole proceedings, playing on the right-hand side of their midfield. He was a less celebrated member of the magnificent French national team of that era, but that cold night in St Etienne, he shone like a beacon. Bundles of skill, allied to non-stop running, we simply couldn't keep him quiet and God knows, 'Cowboy', myself and a few others tried! He was behind the damage that did for us and scored both goals for 'Les Verts'. I regard Larios that night as being the single most difficult opponent I ever faced in my career.

You can see French TV highlights of the game on the internet. Watching it, it was clear that we were playing some good football – when we weren't fighting like lions to keep the French at bay. In fact only a few seconds in and Fronc MahcDoogalle is seen knocking a home player into the night sky. It was typical of Frank - no point in hiding away from them – just let them know you're there. The footage is great, with the commentator seemingly paying special notice to Beelee Thomson, Jean MahCormahck and Beelee Aberchrombee.

After the game our spirits were a wee bit low, as we realised the European adventure had come to an end, just as we were getting a taste for it. Looking back, it was a bit unfortunate to get drawn against as good a team as St Etienne in only the second round and we showed enough over the two legs to suggest that we could have progressed quite far in the competition with a favourable draw. However, what if doesn't count for much in the constantly evolving world of professional football and we soon had to deal with some massive upheaval in our own camp.

Back at the hotel, news came through that the charter flight home, transporting the team, management, directors and club officials, plus the Press had been delayed overnight due to snow. We were being put up in a hotel and Jim Clunie had a word with Jimmy Bone, as it was decided we would have a wee party to mark the end of our UEFA Cup campaign.

The venue was in a few of the rooms occupied by some of the players and as had become the style of JB, it wasn't long before it was in full swing. At some point, the flight crew arrived back at the hotel and having got wind of what was going on, they too joined in the revelry.

Then we got the gatecrashers that nobody wanted - the directors. Big Jim was in one of the rooms and was enjoying letting off steam with the boys. It's fair to say a fair amount of drink had been consumed by all concerned. We had been aware that board/manager relations were not too good, but nobody thought that we would be getting a repeat of the Fergie shambles of two-and-a-half years previously. Wrong.

Something went on during that trip between Jim and the directors. They were not happy at Jim's highly-relaxed state when they came into the room he was in, with a request to keep the noise down. Jim wasn't making much noise – he rarely did. In fact he was probably quieter than when sober. He sat there, quite happily tucking into a massive bag of crisps, while all around him his boys were partying away.

The main problem appeared to be Jim's choice of language. Even under normal circumstances, Jim was a man of few words and every other one seemed to be a swearword. In an advanced state of inebriation, the F-word count was rather higher than normal. It would appear that Jim's version of Tourette's Syndrome was what was upsetting the directors. And to think that celebrity chef Gordon Ramsay has made a career out of the F-word.

A few short hours later at breakfast, Jim was sitting with club director, Gordon Faulds and his wife. Hungover, Jim was as morose as ever and the rude words kept on a comin'. Probably not wise considering his breakfast guest, but surely not that big a deal?

When we finally got on board the plane, we were then informed that due to some complications with the ground crew it would around two to three hours before all the snow and ice could be cleared from the plane, but there was some good news – drinks were being served. Yippee!

Considering how much was probably still in our systems from the night before, it didn't take much to get us rocking again and that applied to the sports journalists who were on board as well. These guys could be trusted and there would be no tabloid tales of the antics, we were sure of that - they would be in their own story.

Jim wasn't really joining in, as he was trying - and failing - to sleep off the night before, so it was left to Ricky to try and stop the plane's bar being drunk dry. He failed. After the promised two to three-hour delay, we were informed that the plane was ready. To be honest, most of the passengers had taken off already.

Just prior to the 'please fasten your seat belts' order being given out, the cabin crew went through the on-board safety instructions, with the able assistance of Alan Logan and myself, dressed up in stewardess outfits and doing all the actions perfectly.

'The emergency exits are located here and here,' we announced complete with exaggerated camp, as we pointed with our hands. Our fellow passengers were in hysterics, as were the cabin crew. While obviously being in breach of aviation rules, the whole episode, including the lengthy bar opening, was enjoyed by all. Maybe not quite all of the passengers. Some of the directors looked incensed by what they had seen, especially with journalists on board - even though the reporters were the most blootered out of the lot of us.

But as we sat on that plane the clock was ticking on Jim Clunie's reign at St Mirren, with yet another superb manager being set on collision course with the esteemed board of directors. This was simply ludicrous, but the next few days were to see this situation get completely out of hand.

On arrival back in Paisley, Jim more or less sealed his fate when he got angry at what was being said on a Radio Clyde phone-in and decided to seek out a public phone to call in and give his views. Unfortunately, he used the F-word live on air and it was broadcast throughout the west of Scotland. Unsurprisingly, this did not go down well with the directors and the atmosphere was worsening.

Where better to go next than Parkhead. However, against all the odds and with a pre-match preparation that was not exactly recommended in any coaching handbook - arriving back late on the Thursday afternoon, most of the squad intoxicated to some extent, the rest with massive hangovers - we came away with a remarkable 2-1 win. Lex Richardson put us 1-0 up with a couple of minutes to go, but Celtic went straight down the other end and got a very dubious penalty which George McCluskey stuck past Billy Thomson. What happened next was totally unexpected by everyone – none more than the St Mirren players.

In injury time, Alex Beckett hit an amazing right-foot volley past Pat Bonner from 25 yards to win the game. I don't think I've ever seen a better struck shot since and it was certainly not the sort of stuff we had expected from Becky. We were overjoyed at the final whistle and trooped off to the dressing rooms to begin the celebrations, unaware of what was about to happen.

The next day, Jim Clunie was sacked as St Mirren manager. Astonishing. The board had gone and done it again. We had just finished third in the league the previous season, had a creditable run in the UEFA Cup and were doing OK in the league. This was obviously down to off the field matters.

My own view is that this was the culmination of a series of events, specifically those surrounding the St Etienne trip and some of the key directors had built up a picture of someone they felt was not a fit and proper person to be the manager. Idiots.

They hired Jim in the first place – did they not do any research on what he was like? Jim was a football man and he knew what made us tick as a team. He knew when to let us let off steam and when to clamp down hard on a lack of discipline. I think the directors were more concerned about their public image - how could we let someone as uncouth as that be manager of OUR team - rather than the performance of the team.

The players were devastated and morale plummeted, especially among those of us who had experienced the Fergie sacking. You began to wonder if the directors actually wanted us to be successful. Only on this occasion, St Mirren were to be very, very lucky. Ricky McFarlane was still Jim's No.2 and he was appointed the manager fairly quickly.

Ricky was a superb coach, widely respected in the professional game, despite not having played at a high level and was definitely ahead of his time. It may sound daft to some, but looking back, Ricky reminds me very much of Arsene Wenger. None of the players had a bad word to say about him, even those who were left out – and that speaks volumes. In fact, during his time as St Mirren manager, he was also manager of Scotland's Under-21 team.

The players were delighted with Ricky's appointment – he was a great man-manager and had demonstrated enough to us already that he would be a success. The trouble was, Ricky's first love was physiotherapy – he was acknowledged as being one of the best in Scotland - and he initially took the job on a temporary basis. The players' response to this was enough to persuade him to take the job permanently and the all-important factor of continuity of a superb managerial/coaching dynasty going back to the Fergie days was maintained.

Shortly after Ricky began his reign, we managed to make a complete mess of the Scottish Cup and were knocked out 2-0 by Dumbarton. However, some enterprising folks at St Mirren managed to organise a one-off match with Arsenal at Love Street. The Gunners had also been victims of a shock early KO in the FA Cup and had a blank weekend in the middle of February. So as not to clash with any cup ties, the game was played on a Sunday afternoon, 15th February 1981 to be precise. A big crowd of about 10,000 piled into Love Street for the friendly and what a game it was.

Peter Weir was in superb form for Saints at this time and was starting to get his full international caps from Jock Stein. A classic measured cross from 'The Sink' saw Big Frank put us 1-0 up and it stayed that way until just after half-time, when Frank Stapleton equalised.

However, Peter soon was on the charge again and he got us back in front, only for David O'Leary to equalise. It was a very strong Arsenal team, with Alan Sunderland and Graham Rix pulling the strings. In the end, Paul Davis scored a late winner for The Gunners, but it was a great game and was terrific entertainment for the Paisley faithful. It went a long way to make up for the Scottish Cup debacle against Dumbarton. St Mirren never really repeated this sort of incentive for an early cup knockout.

The teams that day were - St Mirren: Thomson, Young, Beckett, Richardson, Fulton, Copland, McDougall (Logan), Stark (McCormack), Somner, Abercromby (Bone), Weir.

Arsenal: Jennings (Wood), Devine, Sansom, Talbot (Cox), O'Leary, White, McDermott (Gatting), Sunderland, Stapleton, Davis, Rix.

At the end of the season, one significant transfer took place, when 'The Sink' was sold to Aberdeen and along with some of Fergie's transfer budget, we also got a ready-made replacement - Ian Scanlon.

Ian had played a lot of football in England for Notts County and had been at Pittodrie for Fergie's first title win. He was a supremely skilled left-winger, who also had a good eye for scoring some spectacular goals. Indeed, one of his best-remembered strikes was from fully 40 yards to complete the scoring in a 4-2 win over Celtic at Love Street. We were actually 2-0 down after 20 minutes and the turnaround was truly remarkable.

Ian had a very dry wit and his laid-back delivery of killer one-liners was only beaten by his on-the-field delivery of superb crosses from his left foot. He was a footballing genius who probably never quite got the acclaim that he truly deserved. In that era, only the late Davie Cooper had a better left foot than Ian, he was that good. He was feared by opponents, but stood up to the continual niggling fouls/physical assaults that were sent in his direction. His weakness was a short fuse with referees, whom he felt were not protecting him, or in his competitive mind, were favouring the opposition - as if.

Apart from his obvious attacking threat, Ian was also appreciated by the rest of the team for his ability to take the ball for a walk, giving the rest of us a breather. This tactic usually ended in a foul for St Mirren as well, so it was a popular ploy in the latter stages of games, should we be winning at the time.

The other new face to the squad had come from the less glamorous background of juniors club, Johnstone Burgh. From my neck of the woods in Possil, Milton Man, ex-roadsweeper and apprentice playboy, Frank McAvennie and his then ginger afro began to make his mark at the club very quickly – in his own inimitable fashion.

I had been made aware by some of Saints scouts of Frank's performances for Johnstone Burgh and knew of him from my youth in Possil. I went along to see him play at Keanie Park, home of The Burgh and came back with a glowing report - we could have a real player here, I told everyone at Love Street.

On a professional level, it didn't take Macca long to get into the first team and he was often initially played as an attacking midfielder – but one with a very keen eye for goal. In fact, I think in his first season he was selected for the Scotland Under-21 team, where he scored – naturally - and was voted Young Player of the Year.

A lot has been said about Frank and he was quite a character, with a real zest for life. I think starting the professional game late after a stint as a roadsweeper gave him a different perspective on things from most of his team-mates. He just loved playing football and when he wasn't playing, he just wanted to keep on enjoying himself.

One thing that doesn't get much attention is Macca's bravery. Often playing with his back to goal, Frank would take some real punishment from the opposition, but he kept coming back for more and was never afraid to get stuck in himself.

Frank is often referred to in the media as a Celtic and West Ham legend, but it is to his eternal credit that he always corrects the journalist – particularly if they are Scottish – and insists on St Mirren, Celtic and West Ham legend. The statistics back him up – he spent almost five years at Love Street, playing over 200 matches and scoring 70 goals in the process, placing him in the Top Ten of St Mirren's post-war goalscorers. At the end of 1984-85 season, Frank was sold to West Ham for £340,000 and time was to prove just what a bargain that would be.

Ricky had identified that the defence that had seen us through the last five years was beginning to need a serious overhaul, as injuries and age began to take their toll. At the same time as Frank was making his mark at the club, another outstanding young talent emerged into the first-team, Steve Clarke.

Steve was a genuine class act of a player, initially as full-back, then eventually centre-half. He always seem so composed on the ball, as though nothing would fluster him and it was no surprise that he went on to have a massively successful career at Chelsea following his move there for £400,000 in 1986. But in the early 80s, he was a St Mirren player – and a great colleague. Steve was very quiet, but always extremely focused and determined and did his talking where it mattered, on the pitch.

Steve joined St Mirren in bizarre circumstances, which show how much luck and good fortune can play in shaping the careers of those who make the professional ranks. We were due to play Beith Juniors in a pre-season friendly in 1979, but turned up a week early. A schoolboy Steve was there having a training session and impressed sufficiently to be asked to Love Street for a training session. The rest, as they say, is history.

There were loads of players who came through St Mirren as trialists during my career and many, many of them were better players than me and some of my colleagues. Why did they not make the grade? I put it down to a lack of hunger to succeed. Football was my big shot at escaping from Possil to make a success of my life and I was bloody determined to ensure it would work.

Another addition from the amateur ranks of Queens Park FC at right-back, we saw the emergence of another great player in Tommy Wilson. A great team-mate, on and off the pitch, Tommy was very much an overlapping full-back, who would fly up and down the wings all day long. His inner strength and mental toughness was put to the test early in his career when he suffered a horrendous injury following a tackle at Ibrox by Rangers' Ally Dawson on the opening day of the 83/84 season.

It was a very, very bad challenge, with Dawson's boot crashing through Tommy's knee. Dawson wasn't sent off, unlike Ian Scanlon who had earlier seen red for dissent. I certainly think there was intent, as Tommy had been causing all kinds of problems down Rangers' flank that day. We were all sickened and it looked like his career may be over before it really began. Happily, Tommy came back a year later and went on to star in some of the most memorable games and triumphs that St Mirren had ever known.

To complete the jigsaw, Ricky brought Tony Fitzpatrick back to Love Street from Bristol City for £150,000. It speaks volumes for Tony's enduring affection for St Mirren that he chose to re-sign for Saints, despite strong interest from Celtic and Aberdeen.

In retrospect, Ricky had managed a minor miracle, in being able to replace long-term key figures in the squad, such as John Young and Jackie Copland, who were coming to the end of their careers, with great young talent and still not affect the progress that St Mirren had been making. Despite the mayhem surrounding his appointment, Ricky still managed to steer us to a fifth place finish in 1981/82 and we matched this the following season, when Ricky's old pal Fergie was to do St Mirren a massive favour by proxy, even though that was probably the furthest thing from his mind…..

In May 1983, Aberdeen won the European Cup Winners Cup with a 2-1 win against Real Madrid, after extra time.. This was a truly remarkable feat and one which was applauded by the rest of Scottish football – no more than at Love Street, as Aberdeen's triumph meant that our fifth place finish meant that an extra UEFA Cup slot was available and we were back in Europe as a consequence. When Peter Weir set up John Hewitt's winner, he probably had no idea how much it was celebrated by his old colleagues in Paisley.

ABER'S GONNAE GET YE!

Realistically, we weren't expecting to win the UEFA Cup, but a nice run, possibly ending after three or four rounds against one of Europe's leading clubs, would have been an achievable aim.

Unfortunately, the draw was to be less than kind. We were to play Feyenoord with the first leg in Paisley. Following my two yellow cards collected against Elfsborg and St.Etienne, I knew that I was under a UEFA one-match ban, so my heart sank. This was as tough a draw as you could have wished for. Among Feyenoord's squad was the young up and coming star Ruud Gullit and the not-so-young, but still in a different league to the rest of us, Johann Cruyff.

A tight defensive performance was the aim as we kicked-off the first leg amidst yet another Paisley monsoon. Tommy Wilson had suffered that terrible injury against Rangers just a few weeks earlier and Stevie Clarke had shifted from left-back to right-back, with Phil McAveety coming in at left-back. Phil had been on the fringes of the St Mirren team since 1977 and you have to admire his spirit and patience for still being around the fringes of the team six years later.

Phil was an extremely likeable big lump and a bit of a comedian – even though he was not aware of this talent. Perhaps he was kept on the books that long purely to keep spirits high amongst everyone, including his young colleagues in the reserves. Phil did a great job that night, along with the rest of the guys – Steve Clarke in particular - and we were unfortunate to lose 1-0 to a deflected Ruud Gullit goal. Little was Steve to know that he would be working beside Ruud in years to come at Chelsea and Newcastle United.

Not long after the home leg, my old pal Lex Richardson was sold to Dundee in a straight swap for the Dark Blues' highly-rated striker, Eric Sinclair. I had known that Lex had been wanting a move for a variety of reasons, but it was sad to see him go after all the years we had spent together at Love Street.

As for Eric Sinclair, the move was a disaster. He never fitted in at Love Street either on the pitch, among the rest of the players, or with the supporters who were just as sad to see Lexy go – he was a hard act to follow. Given Lexy's performances through his career at St Mirren and the almost non-appearance of any sustainable form from Eric, everyone got the feeling that St Mirren had been done over by Dundee in the deal.

If you thought that a pattern was forming here – St Mirren yet to score at home in a European tie and playing the games in horrendous Paisley weather, then the events surrounding the return leg would confirm your suspicions.

Incredibly, the managerial hot seat at Love Street was starting to warm-up again. On this occasion it wasn't the board's decision, but that of Ricky himself and a large portion of the blame could be heaped on elements of the St Mirren support and the media.

St Mirren had achieved a phenomenal rise in their fortunes in the previous six years, but by now and in some parts of the support and the Press this success was becoming automatically expected, as opposed to being encouraged and celebrated. This was ludicrous, given the size of the club and its support base, in relation to Aberdeen, Celtic and Rangers. At this point in Scottish football, Dundee United were achieving wonders under Jim McLean and this may have added to the expectation at Love Street, as we were now firmly part of the Top Five, in Scotland.

However, all the usual boring, but evil necessity stuff like finances, were putting a strain on Saints' abilities to keep up this position. At the start of 1983-84 our hardcore home support was probably just under 4000. We didn't get off to a particularly strong start that season and we didn't claim a league win until the end of October, when Rangers were thumped 3-0 at Love Street.

Fortunately, in the interim period, we had amassed enough draws to ensure that we were not in any trouble. However, newly promoted Hearts - with a certain Jimmy Bone, who had signed for Hearts after leaving Saints in the summer of 1982 scoring regularly for them - looked to be taking our place among the Top Five and some of the natives were getting restless. In addition, Fergie had raided us again for Billy Stark and Billy was in fine form for The Dons. All of this was building pressure on Ricky and I felt that he was getting very unfair treatment from some of the fans and certainly from some of the Press. In the end, I think Ricky thought he didn't really need all the hassle and decided to quit.

In September 1983, on the morning of the game in Rotterdam, Ricky let a few of the senior pros know of his plans and we were devastated. Given his reasons, you couldn't help but feel that we had let him down, but Ricky was having none of it. He firmly reaffirmed his view that the bloated expectancy had meant that he simply didn't enjoy being St Mirren manager any more.

ABER'S GONNAE GET YE!

Ricky asked us not to let the rest of the squad, who were a bit younger and less experienced, know what was going to happen, as he didn't want them distracted from the game that night. We felt that we owed Ricky a good performance for all the good times we had under his guidance and boy did we give it a good go against Cruyff and Co in De Kuip stadium.

I returned to midfield and Cowboy was moved in beside me. The brief was simple – try and keep Cruyff and Gullit quiet, break up their creative midfield and stop Feyenoord getting any fluency going.

Big Phil McAveety played the game of his career as we kept them at bay with a brave and committed performance, occasionally breaking away ourselves, with Macca and Big Frank looking lively. An away goal would have completely changed the mood of the crowd and the tone of Feyenoord's approach, but it was not to be.

On the hour, Van Til hit a long-range strike past Billy Thomson and things started to look bleak. We kept pressing, but as happens in these situations, we got punished for opening up from our policy of contain and break and Jeliazkov – set up by Gullit - scored with ten minutes to go to make it 2-0. As the game had opened up, Gullit enjoyed the freedom and played the last 30 minutes as if he was in slippers, effortlessly gliding up and down the right-hand side, almost prancing about when he got the ball. He was an unknown talent then on the European stage – this was about to change.

The late goal was tough to take. We had battled so hard over the two legs, that the 3-0 aggregate didn't give a true reflection of our contribution of the tie. Also, it was doubly frustrating that our Euro dream was over after only one round, due to a very tough draw, while less able teams than St Mirren were being drawn against part-timers from the lesser known European leagues.

This frustration manifested itself in the considerable shape of Frank McDougall, who was sent off with Feyenoord's Van der Korput following an off the ball incident. Handbags was the general term for the wee squabble, but Frank landed one on the Dutchman that Mr. Van der Korput wouldn't forget in a hurry. The only light moment came when all the home fans started laughing as Frank was walking up the tunnel - the wrong tunnel. There was one for the home team and one for the visitors, each tunnel going straight to the dressing rooms. When Frank emerged from the home tunnel a few seconds later, the stadium erupted in laughter and cheering. This didn't help Frank's dark mood one iota and the subject was avoided until many hours after the game.

Returning from Rotterdam, the news broke that Ricky had quit. Now we had a big problem – previous changes to the team manager had been filled quickly and credit where it is due, had been filled well. The resignation came as a big surprise for the board and unlike previous appointments where they may well have had time to plan who the next manager would be, this was not a luxury available this time.

We were heading into a busy winter schedule and the ship needed to be steadied – otherwise the consequence could be fairly dire. Although, a truly awful Motherwell side did seem to be trying their best to be relegated by March.

In the interim period, Ricky's trusted lieutenants, Eddie MacDonald and Erik Sorensen looked after the team, acting as dual caretakers - only at St Mirren could you get dual caretaker managers.

Eddie was a close friend of Ricky's and we thought that he would be gone when the new boss was appointed. Erik was a highly entertaining individual, with striking Scandinavian looks and rigorous approach to fitness and discipline that certainly stood out among his Scottish charges. He used to bark out orders in his clipped Scandinavian tones, which did make him sound slightly like a German Officer at a POW camp: 'Ve hav vays of getting you vit Aber'.

He was completely correct in his approach and it was a good alternative to the more laid back approach from Ricky and Eddie. I'll give Erik this - despite the players' best efforts, we were about the fittest team in Scotland while he was there and this went a long way to help a small squad perform well over a long season.

The appointment of a new manager was made just as the wheels were threatening to come off the Saints lorry, with a 5-0 thrashing at Ibrox in the League Cup. Former Rangers full-back Alex Miller had been doing very well down the M8 at county rivals Morton as player/manager and he was signed up by St Mirren on the day of the Rangers game. Alex prepared his Morton team for their fixture that evening, before zipping along the motorway to Govan to watch his new charges get right royally gubbed. This strange start was only the beginning of an eventful three-year reign by Alex Miller at St Mirren.

6 It's Miller Time

ALEX Miller had all the right ingredients to be a top manager. He was extremely professional and well-organised and he seemed to live for the game – it was a consuming passion for him and there were shades of Fergie in him, that's for sure. The fact that he is still involved at the highest level, assisting Rafa Benitez, at Liverpool before going on to manage Japanese club JEF United Chiba speaks volumes for Alex's drive and dedication. Purely on a personal level, it is fair to say that we had our differences, but this doesn't diminish my professional respect for Alex Miller.

He was often very thorough in his tactical briefings to the team prior to kick-off with the sole exception of myself. Alex just used to say: 'Aber - No. 4.' No further instructions were given and you can read into this whatever you want. This was actually quite a compliment from Alex, as he was putting quite a bit of responsibility for the team performance on me and believed in my abilities. I think he appreciated my personal strengths, even though our relationship was often stormy.

On one occasion, I was almost late for kick-off in a match at Love Street. I wasn't driving at the time and had taken the bus, even getting an early one just to make sure. There was an incident on the way to the ground and I arrived at 2.40pm to find Alex going apoplectic with rage. 'Where the f**k have you been? What f*****g time is this?'

I replied: 'I'm sorry boss, but a building fell down in front of me.'

This was actually true, as a tenement had collapsed in front of the bus. Clearly, Alex thought I was taking the piss and could barely manage a coherent sentence, going red with rage and nearly choking as he shouted: 'What? What f*****g building? Collapsing? Shite - just get f*****g changed and get out there.' I think this was the only time he expanded beyond my pre-match 'Number…' instruction.

ABER'S GONNAE GET YE!

One problem that Alex had was that in his early weeks as manager he kept on making reference to his career at Rangers .(He'd been 15 years as a player, winning all domestic trophies, plus the European Cup Winners Cup. If we heard 'When I was at Rangers' once, we must have heard it a thousand times. Personally, it just washed off me – I just tuned in to the important football related information, but the constant harping on about Rangers did get on the nerves of some of the players, in particular Frank McAvennie. This was not because Macca was a Celtic fan, but because he was of the clear belief that 'Rangers have f**k all to do with St Mirren'. Straightforward Milton logic at its best, Macca.

Also, in the early 80s we had been on the bad end of some controversial defeats to Rangers, some games of which did involve Alex Miller, so you could understand how some of the lads got annoyed at the Ibrox references. Ricky had been a players man and it was quickly evident that this was not Alex's style. A bad atmosphere began to develop and a clear-the-air meeting was held between Alex and the senior pros. It was real cards on the table stuff and you have to credit Alex for having the bottle to call the meeting. It worked and from that point on, the whole mood lightened and we began to progress on the pitch as well.

We didn't always make life easy for Alex or ourselves and it was Paris that was the root of the problem. Not the capital of France and the global capital of romance, but Paris the neon-lit nightclub that was the Paisley cornerstone of the players' social scene in the early 80s.

Wednesday night was Paris night and it was the scene of most of our unprofessional moments that used to drive Alex daft. It got to the point where he tried to ban us from the place.

One night, Macca and Big Frank McDougall - Possil's very own answer to Miami Vice's Crockett and Tubbs - pitched up in the standard regalia of shiny suits and in Macca's case, peroxide highlights. They ordered the usual two pints of lager - Macca's taste for champagne had remained undiscovered in Paisley's nightspots - although there was a bar called "Stringfellows" behind the ground. The happy lads turned round to see what sexy young things were up on the dancefloor shaking their stuff to the latest from Duran Duran. Instead, what they saw was Alex Miller standing at the end of the bar, the neon making him look like he was wearing the original Technicolour Raincoat. 'Right ya pair of idiots. I f*****g warned you. You'll never play for this club* again!'

ABER'S GONNAE GET YE!

* (I presume that he meant St Mirren, not Paris).

Now we were a good team, but not so good as to sell our top strikers on account of a Wednesday night out. The Two Franks stayed put and carried on firing in the goals.

Unsurprisingly, I was to fall foul of Mr. Miller regarding Paris, but ironically it was in the mildest of circumstances given some of the excesses committed by us in the place.

In the early part of 1984/85 season we were knocked out of the League Cup 2-0 by Cowdenbeath, at Central Park. This was a very, very bad result and a breathtakingly inept performance by us. The mood on the way home was very quiet and we were all pretty embarrassed by what had just happened.

The team bus dropped us off at Love Street at about 11.30pm and Macca, veteran reserve keeper Jim Stewart and myself decided to go to Paris for a swift half before heading home. It was so late that only the one drink was possible, so any thoughts of a rip-roaring night out were far from our minds.

Unfortunately for us there were also some St Mirren supporters in the place, who had also just got back from Fife. Already in a dark mood from the performance from their heroes at Cowdenbeath, these boys were even less impressed to see three of the players in a nightclub after the game. The actual circumstances were not quite as bad as that would appear, but you can see how it looked to them. The three of us left after our one drink, blissfully unaware of what was to happen the next day.

Accompanying the headlines concerning the shock result, were reports that 'St Mirren stars, Billy Abercromby, Frank McAvennie and Jim Stewart were seen drinking the night away in a Paisley nightclub a few hours later'. The disgruntled fans must have tipped off the Press and Alex Miller's reaction was volcanic. We were all fined two weeks' wages, making the round of three shandies the most expensive in Scottish history.

One person who had a massive bust-up with the manager, that wasn't Paris-related, was Billy Thomson. Billy had been increasingly frustrated by contract negotiations between St Mirren and himself and seemed to think that Alex was not helping the situation. Things came to an abrupt end when Billy went public with his grievances.

Alex Miller went berserk and said that Billy would never play for St

Mirren again. On this occasion, his threat wasn't empty. Billy never did play for St Mirren again and one of the greatest goalkeepers to have played for the club was soon sold to Dundee United for a bargain basement £75,000 while still at the peak of his powers. The gaffer's decision-making here did have a safety net; whereas there was no way he could have afforded to boot out McAvennie and McDougall, Billy had a superb understudy, primed and ready to fill the goalkeeper's jersey.

Campbell Money would go on to be arguably the greatest post-war goalkeeper for St Mirren, clocking up over 400 appearances in the process. Known as Dibble on account of him being a Policeman before he went full-time, Campbell certainly was an officer and a gentleman. The big man was a really genuine guy and he used to take the results to heart more than any other player. He was desperate for St Mirren to do well and ended up playing out his entire career at Love Street.

Dibble got a couple of Under-21 caps and was a regular member of Scotland squads under Stein and Roxburgh, but they both preferred either Jim Leighton or Alan Rough. The latter was certainly at the end of his career and Campbell must have been disappointed to be overlooked in favour of Roughie – but he never let it show.

Alex Miller soon started to bring his own choice of players into the squad and to be fair, these were largely excellent signings that would make the framework of the team that went on to finally realise the hopes and ambitions of St Mirren supporters a few years later.

First man in was full-back Derek Hamilton, signed from Aberdeen. 'Moon Man' was most definitely a 'one-off'. He fancied himself as the next Rod Stewart and seriously claimed to be a better singer, requiring very little encouragement to demonstrate this to anyone who would listen. It took a few orbits to get on to whatever planet Derek was on, but when you got there, then you found one of the warmest, funniest people you could hope to meet.

Derek and I bonded well and he quickly became a fully paid-up member of the dressing room Corner Gang. What many people don't know is that he was a fanatical trainer - possibly to work off the excesses from the weekend/midweek refuelling sessions and was obsessed with maintaining his admirable stamina and boxer's physique. There wasn't a spare piece of flesh on him and it was this dedication which possibly distracted managerial attention concerning Derek's off the field antics - which would

ABER'S GONNAE GET YE!

have been enough to give Alex a heart attack if he knew half of what went on.

On more than one occasion after a midweek game, Derek and I stayed in the Players' Lounge, at Love Street until everybody had gone. The staff left with a cheery wave and our promise to lock up and leave the keys in a safe place. We then set about refreshing ourselves into the wee small hours, before kipping on the floor, in a very deep sleep. In the morning, we let ourselves out, left the keys in the safe place as promised and were unsurprisingly first ones in for training, stripped and changed before anyone else arrived. This dedication seemed to impress the blissfully unaware Mr. Miller.

One day, we pushed our luck too far though and the recriminations came from a higher level than the St Mirren management team. After training Derek and I were driving out to Lochwinnoch where I was living at the time. Derek would drop me off before he headed home to nearby Beith. We stopped for a pub lunch in Howood. Two chicken and chips, several hours and ten-plus pints of Guinness later, we made the stupid decision to set off on the second leg of our journey - with Moon Man at the wheel of his car.

We barely went 200 yards, before Derek lost control and careered right through a hedge and straight through a greenhouse. Dusting ourselves down, we got out the car and realised it was a wreck. Fortunately, nobody was at home as it was still only late afternoon, so we made our escape plans.

I decided to walk it home over a back road that I knew, but Derek, with a wee bit further to travel, decided that he would hitch a lift a few hundred yards down the road. The next morning, there was no sign of Derek at training, but I had to mask my concern to my colleagues: 'He seemed OK when I left him yesterday', was my line with the rest of the players and management remaining unaware of what had gone on.

I finally tracked him down later that night at his house in Beith. Turns out that Derek had managed to flag a lift down and as they drove off, Derek opened up with his trademark: 'Alright, kids?', before telling them all of what had happened and how he needed to get out of the area before the police arrived.

At this point, the driver smiled, slowed down and flashed a badge at Derek. The stupid sod had only thumbed a lift from an unmarked police car containing two CID officers from Mill Street Police HQ in Paisley.

Charges of drink driving and fleeing the scene of an accident were soon successfully prosecuted, with a 12 month driving ban and a £200 fine.

One week after Derek signed, Alex Miller signed Neil Cooper, from Grimsby. His first game at centre-half was the previously mentioned game at Love Street against Celtic, where we were 2-0 down inside 20 minutes, only to go on and win 4-2. It was an amazing match and one that still gets mentioned in articles on the greatest game seen at Love Street. Neil was a very accomplished ball-playing centre-half, who could read the game beautifully. It was like having Willie Miller in the team – apart from the fact that Neil didn't referee games while playing in them.

Other additions to the defence were the home grown talents of Dave Winnie and the striking figure of Peter 'Basil' Godfrey. David was what is referred to as a cultured centre-half, although initially he started as a left-back. He had a great left foot and always seemed to be composed and focused, despite his young age when he broke into the first team. He was a very quiet lad and getting a word out of him was bloody difficult – he made Steve Clarke look like a motormouth in comparison.

Big Peter was signed from Meadowbank Thistle after he had impressed against us in a marathon Scottish Cup tie against Meadowbank Thistle that went to two replays. Known as 'Basil' due to his status as a Basil Fawlty lookalike, Peter was a real gentleman, straightforward and always with a big smile for everyone.

He used to get all manner of stick from the corner gang in the dressing room, but he just let it go way over his head and carried on smiling. He used to go on rampaging runs from his centre-half position, knocking opponents over like skittles, heading from penalty area to penalty area in a straight line. It was great to watch when you were on the pitch and must have been massively entertaining for fans of both sides.

Finally, young winger Gardner Speirs made the transition from the reserves through to the first team squad. Gardner was a brilliant striker of the ball and a genuine raw talent in his early career at Love Street. He was known as 'Scoop', which was a fairly cruel nickname. He had developed a habit of beating opponents with skill and pace, before getting into a scoring position and scooping the ball over the bar.

Gardner tried to work on this at training, like any pro should, but this was to make the problem worse, largely due to his team-mates. We would mercilessly take the piss out of him during training for his scoops and the

ABER'S GONNAE GET YE!

more we said it, the more he did it. By Friday's sessions at Abbotsinch, his attempts on goal were troubling the air traffic controllers, at nearby Glasgow Airport. Despite our best/worst efforts, Gardner broke the habit and became a valued member of the team and a member of the Left Peg Culture Club that I used to wind him up about at training.

The honorary member of this club was myself - naturally, as what is the point in creating such a thing if you cannot include yourself - with the other members being Davie Cooper, 'Lexy', 'The Sink' and 'Scan'. When I told Gardner that he made my club, it was a great compliment from a senior pro to a youngster coming through and I think he appreciated it. Alex Miller would probably have had me sectioned under the Mental Health Act.

There is no doubt that Alex Miller not only stabilised Saints that season, but quickly managed to strengthen the team and get us back on the forward momentum again. We only just missed out on a UEFA Cup place, finishing sixth, but considering the awful first half of the season, this was no disgrace and a sign that we were looking good for the next season.

While almost the entire defence was re-built, the Possil-powered frontline of Macca and Big Frank was becoming feared by all opposition, with Fitzy and Ian Scanlon providing the ammo. Our optimism was not misplaced. At the end of Miller's first season in charge, the two Franks were separated – finally when 'Luther' was sold to Aberdeen for £100,000. This was to prove to be a nice piece of business – again - by Fergie as Frank went on to score the goals that brought Aberdeen almost every piece of silverware available in Scotland over the next couple of years, before a chronic back injury cruelly forced him to retire aged just 28, just after he won the European Golden Boot.

Miller brought in two strikers to replace the big fella – Brian Gallagher and Kenny McDowall. A natural poacher of goals, 'Gal' was a comedian and everything was a complete joke to Brian.

He had a great attitude to life and his unique frame of mind was a great boost around the dressing room. He was the ultimate wind-up merchant and no one was safe. My own undoing from 'Gal's' pranks just about summed up the way there were no limits to his methodology.

After an away trip in Prague, 'Gal' and a few of the boys went out in the historic city for a few beers to unwind after a successful match - more of which later. Normally, I would have been at the vanguard of such a trip, but I was absolutely knackered, having played the game with an injury and missing some of the previous league matches for the same reason.

By the time the boys came back suitably re-hydrated - and we are not talking isotonic here - 'Gal' had hit on another idea for a wind-up and I was to be the victim.

From YTS trainees to senior pros, 'Gal' didn't give a flying one – we were all fair game. By now, I was in a complete state of unconsciousness, but unwisely, I was lying on top of the covers in the buff, due to the searing temperatures in the hotel.

Fortunately, I was lying on my front – but this didn't present a problem for Mr. Gallagher who managed to quietly gain access to my room, with his accomplices. Somehow he had procured some burning powder - a kind of 50/50 mix between itching powder and granulated Ralgex - and liberal quantities were applied where the sun don't shine on your truly. A couple of minutes later, I awoke from my slumbers to what can only be described as an excruciating burning sensation in an area that I will leave to your imagination.

As I started jumping around the room, screams getting louder, I became aware of a mop of curly hair silhouetted in the half-light of the room. It was shaking with barely suppressed laughter. 'Gaaaaaall ! You f*****g baaastard! OOOOH ! OOOOH ! What have you done ya f*****g maniac!'

When he wasn't devising ways of humiliating/torturing his team-mates, Brian was also a very good footballer and a scorer of many an opportunistic goal.

Kenny 'Kojak' McDowall was brought in from Partick Thistle in 1984 and stayed ten years with St Mirren for the rest of his playing career. Kenny was a great lad – one of the good guys. He was a very committed striker and a real handful for anyone unlucky enough to play against him. I am very glad that I never had to play against him, although our training ground clashes were tasty enough in themselves.

Kenny didn't take any nonsense from anyone and defenders knew it. Any centre-half daft enough to try and dish it out to Kenny would get it back - with interest. This kind of intimidation was good for the team and we all appreciated his efforts.

It is hardly surprising that two of the things Kenny's playing career at Love Street was remembered for were a) scoring the only goal at Ibrox in a 1-0 win on the opening day of the season, where he crashed through Chris Woods as they both went for a cross ball. TV replays showed the goal to be fair, but Woods being helped off with a broken collarbone didn't exactly brighten Graeme Souness' mood; and b) the attempted decapitation of a KV Mechelen player during a European Cup Winners Cup Tie. The Belgian lad had fouled Kenny from behind and right in front of the BBC cameras, Kenny basically tried to remove the guys head from his shoulders with a well-aimed back-heel. Somehow he never got punished for this.

It may surprise some, but Kenny was a great listener, keen to improve his game and learn about new tactics and techniques. It is no surprise to see him now regarded as an excellent coach having spent several successful years at Celtic before moving on to the other side of the Old Firm, Rangers.

Sadly, 'Cowboy' - another member of the old Possil Crew - was sold off to Dundee. His replacement was the highly-experienced combative midfielder Jim Rooney, signed from Morton. Despite his Greenock connections, the St Mirren support soon took to Jim's committed style of play. We used to call him 'Caspar' on account of the way he used to ghost into the opposition box – they were probably astonished to see him that far up the park. Jim wasn't afraid to get stuck in and was very similar to me. Although he was not quite up to my levels of commitment.

Part of the 'Cowboy' transfer saw the arrival at Love Street of Dundee's attacking midfielder Peter Mackie. Peter had one big problem - as good a player as he was, he wasn't as good a player as he thought he was. It was like he thought he was Kenny Dalglish. There was a very slight physical resemblance and he often wore the No.7 shirt, but that is where the similarity ended. He did have some good moments for us, but I think that his spell at Love Street was not the success story that he, nor Alex Miller, had thought it would be.

Although a couple of the prime movers had left our very own Rat Pack, we still had a great off-the-park social scene going with Paisley bar, Jack Daniels, in New Street being our main designated meeting point for discussions on the ever-changing political scene of the 80s. That last bit isn't quite true, but you can use your imagination, multiply it by ten and you might be getting close.

It is fair to say that we weren't a bunch of choir boys – but we did the business on the pitch and that is what counts. It was around this time that St Mirren used to take part in the Isle of Man Summer Cup, a pre-season tournament, with a mix of a couple of Scottish teams, a couple of English teams and a local side. Playing against the likes of Bolton Wanderers and Coventry City was a fun way to limber up for the campaign and this was shared by the St Mirren support. Lots of fans would travel down to the island for their summer holidays, by day taking in the games and in the evenings joining in the festivities with the players. These were smashing trips and there was a kind of laid-back innocence about those days that seems to be sadly missing from the game today.

Alex Miller's first full season in charge - 1984-85 - saw this unit of players play consistently well and we finished fifth to secure another crack at European football. The draw once again was unkind and we were drawn against Czech side Slavia Prague – only this time we would have second leg home advantage.

Most of the lads had European experience from our European adventure two years previous, but it still didn't amount to what could be described as a valuable amount. Fortunately, St Mirren had re-signed Frank McGarvey from Celtic and during his stay there, Frank had amassed a lifetime of Euro knowledge and being true to form, he wasn't afraid to let us all know what we should be doing in these games and the situations they throw up.

The first leg saw Saints wear an all-blue kit, hastily arranged from a Paisley sports shop just prior to leaving for Eastern Europe. At that time, our home top was basically all-white, with the famous black stripes being replaced by thin pinstripes - it was all the rage I can assure you. The away kit was all red. What colours did Slavia Prague play in? Red and white tops. Therefore, a badgeless, sponsorless St Mirren turned up for another crack at the UEFA Cup.

If the locals thought they were up against a bunch of amateurs from Scotland, they were mistaken as we fought a brave rearguard action for virtually the entire 90 minutes in a narrow 1-0 defeat for us.

I had been carrying an injury, but Alex Miller made it clear that he wanted me in midfield that night, believing that my style of play was perfect for that sort of game. To be fair, he gave me a lot of credit in the Press after the game and while players mostly get embarrassed in being singled out by a manager for praise - mainly due to the rest of the dressing-room taking the p**s out of them as a consequence - I did appreciate his comments.

For me, the real star that night was Campbell Money. 'Dibble' was utterly immense and was able to cope with virtually everything Slavia threw at him, with a performance that really put down his mark as being the best young keeper in Scotland.

I remember that a couple of St Mirren fans had made it all the way from Paisley to Prague by hitch-hiking and although they couldn't have made any impact on the partisan local support, their presence was impressive, to put it mildly.

Some of the major clubs attract massive travelling support throughout Europe, which is commendable. However, at a provincial club, there seems to be a closer connection between the players and the support. You kind of get the impression that we were all in it together, trying to achieve our best against all the odds. Their devotion to the cause, often in the face of any logic other than this is their team should never be sneered at. I can assure you that players do appreciate the backing of a loyal support – irrespective of its numbers. Size isn't everything - apparently.

Although no away goal was scored, we still felt we had a great chance back at Love Street. The second leg was a pulsating affair, played in front of about 12,000 at a very, very noisy Love Street. Sadly, I was injured and played no part, as goals from 'Gal' and Frank McGarvey (2) saw St Mirren go through 3-1 after extra time. Joking apart, it was a game that was made for Frank and his European pedigree came to the fore. If anyone had told him that nine years after joining Division 1 St Mirren from Kilwinning Rangers, he would be back at Love Street scoring crucial goals in a UEFA Cup win over Slavia Prague, then Frank would have believed them - and tried to make a bet on it happening as well.

The draw for the second round again gave us home advantage in the second leg. This time we were drawn against Swedish side Hammarby, about whom we knew next to bugger all. The injury I was carrying in Prague was still keeping me out, but I was a proud onlooker as Gal scored a hat-trick in a 3-3 draw - this was some feat and his record for being a Scot scoring an away hat-trick in European competition stood for many, many years to come. Conceding three is never clever, but with away goals counting double, we were in a positive frame of mind for the game in Paisley.

ABER'S GONNAE GET YE!

Just prior to the return leg at Love Street on the 6th November, both Rangers and Celtic were knocked out of their own European campaigns. The scene was set. If we could capitalise on our 3-3 away leg, then not only would St Mirren make it to the third round of the UEFA Cup for the first time ever, but we would be the sole representatives of the West of Scotland.

This would have meant belated high levels of media interest, plus a bumper crowd to match. If we got a soft draw, then we could be looking at a run to the semis. Everyone was in buoyant, optimistic mood – but completely focused on getting the job done.

A good crowd of more than 11,000 were in good voice and this was enhanced when Frank McGarvey put us 1-0 up. I had come on earlier as a sub for Jim Rooney and the message was clear - all we had to do was keep the game tight and all would be well. Frank was substituted with about five minutes to go, to rapturous applause. Then things went very, very wrong indeed.

In the 89th minute Hammarby equalised at the Love Street end. I thought 'OK don't panic, we're still through, just a few minutes to go…'

In injury time, the Swedes broke through again and despite a late lunge from Tommy Wilson, the striker fired past 'Dibble'. The ref blew his whistle and pointed towards the penalty box. I thought he had given a penalty, but amazingly, he gave us a free-kick, presumably for a non-existent offside against the Swedish striker.

By now bedlam had descended; with the noise of St Mirren fans whistling for full-time almost deafening the players, Hammarby smelled blood, despite their being only seconds left on the clock. For some inexplicable reason - and there were plenty of experienced pros in the Saints team that night - we rushed the free-kick and quickly conceded possession. As the clock edged towards the last ten seconds of injury-time, Hammarby cut through our defence, every Saints player moving as though in quicksand as panic shredded our concentration. Everything seemed to go into slow-motion and when the ball slowly crept past Dibble for the third time in two minutes, I felt sick. From the restart, the ball didn't even get out of the centre-circle before the ref blew for time up.

The biggest disappointment of my playing career by a country mile had just been achieved.

As we trooped into the dressing room in stunned silence, we found Frank McGarvey sitting there feeling quite pleased with himself. When we told him what had just happened, he initially thought it was a wind-up. The ashen faces of all the players and the coaching staff soon made him change his mind and soon after he was in tears.

He wasn't the only one. It was a terrible body blow for the club and the players and it took us months to get over. The players and fans who were there that night were definitely mentally scarred by the sickening turns of emotion and it was the fans that I really felt for. This was their chance to really be proud of their team on a European stage, especially in light of the Old Firm's elimination. And we let them down.

The next morning Alex had us in for some light training at Love Street and the mood was one of numb shock. Nobody wanted to say anything or to point any finger of blame – it would have started a riot in the dressing room. To use the old cliché, you could have cut the atmosphere with a knife. There was so much anger, frustration, humiliation and disappointment being felt by each and every member of the squad. The silence was deafening, and it was as if a huge storm was about to break over us. Alex decided to just get us out and run some laps around the park, probably to burn off the nervous tension.

What I will never forget is that when we went to do some jogging around the pitch, the track was littered with discarded scarves and programmes, thrown away in anger and crushing disappointment. We all saw the debris and barely a word was spoken. At that point in my career, this was as low as I had ever felt.

7 Always The Bridesmaid

HOW close we came to winning the Premier League in 1980 reinforced the belief among the players that silverware could be ours. Realistically, the League title was a big ask, but the League Cup or Scottish Cup were achievable aims. However, St Mirren's attempts at achieving cup glory in the early part of the 1980s were to be the definition of footballing heartbreak.

In the 1981-82 season, we got to the semi-final of the League Cup. It was a two-legged affair and we were drawn against Rangers, against whom we fancied our chances, although this optimism was not shared by the media – maybe they knew something we didn't. The first leg was at Love Street and ended in a very entertaining 2-2 draw, with a superb solo effort from Macca and an Ian Scanlon penalty being our counters. We had enough of the play to believe that an upset could be achieved two weeks later, at Ibrox.

In the second leg, we were 1-0 up by half-time, thanks to a Tony Fitzpatrick penalty, but a worrying marker had been put down when Jimmy Bone had a perfectly good goal disallowed for a dubious offside against Lex Richardson. I say dubious as there was the small matter of a couple of Rangers players on the goal line.

We should have been two goals clear with only 45 minutes between us and a League Cup Final appearance, at Hampden. It was soon to go badly wrong. Straight after half-time, Lex was put through and as he was about to go round Jim Stewart, Rangers' veteran centre-half Colin Jackson blatantly took him out. These days it would be a professional foul and a straight red card, but that night referee George Smith waved play on. Truly astonishing and we began to lose momentum as a series of strange decisions went against us. This culminated in John 'Polaris' MacDonald once again popping down his periscope when 'Cowboy' decided to make the rash decision of coming within coughing distance of him. Down he went and unsurprisingly Smith needed little encouragement in pointing to the spot and Jim Bett slotted away the equaliser.

We lost the place completely and all shape and focus went out the window with our sense of injustice, which in retrospect was unprofessional. With less than five minute to go, the final nail in the coffin was hammered in by, who else but 'Polaris', this time actually finishing from open play - for a change. I couldn't stand the wee diving b*****d and if the game had gone on a couple of minutes longer, I swear I would have broken his leg, such was my anger. I make no apologies for admitting this, for despite being a professional, the guys who blatantly cheated with their diving used to really get to me and in the circumstances at Ibrox, my red mist was well and truly down.

Fortunately, the final whistle spared the inevitable clash. As a barometer of how dodgy the refereeing was television commentator Archie MacPherson said during the highlights that St Mirren were very unlucky and the victims of some questionable refereeing to put it mildly. Cheers Archie.

We never really did anything again of note in the League Cup during my career at Love Street. Instead, a grim tale of always the bridesmaid, but never the bride ensued in successive ill-fated attempts to win the big one – The Scottish Cup.

A few months after the League Cup Semis, we worked our way to the semi-final of the Scottish Cup, where we met Aberdeen at Parkhead. It was a fairly dour, tight affair, until a moment of controversy put St Mirren 1-0 up with less than half an hour to play. Big Frank ploughed into Jim Leighton going for a cross and Jim let the ball go from his grasp and it slid just wide of the post. Aberdeen felt, possibly with good grounds, that it was a free-kick, but as they carried on arguing, the resulting corner went through to Cowboy, who slipped it to Big Frank to rifle home.

Aberdeen went mental at the injustice, not least Fergie, who was suitably enraged on the sidelines. A few minutes later Billy Thomson was adjudged to have brought down Mark McGhee. It was a soft decision at best and perhaps referee Hugh Alexander was looking to even things up after Frank's goal. Gordon Strachan slotted away the penalty and this was perhaps a bit too much for me to take, given my ongoing battles with him.

Soon afterwards, Strachan knocked the ball past me and I launched into him with what was a hopelessly late tackle. It was right in front of the dugouts and Fergie and his gang were racing out to remonstrate with the officials. I was already booked and didn't hang about to see the red card being waved. Immediately, I was worried that I had cost us the chance of getting to Hampden – it was still 1-1 after all. The boys held on and four days later the teams met again at Dens Park.

Despite the relatively dull encounter a few days earlier and the fact that it was raining in Biblical proportions on Tayside, the replay was to be a very exciting, open match.

Mark McGhee struck first, with the ball slipping through Billy Thomson's grasp, putting us 1-0 down inside ten minutes. Not a great start, but Macca soon equalised, nipping in between Miller and Leighton, who both seemed to be stuck in the deepening Dens Park mud as the incessant rain got heavier, to prod home the loose ball. Before half-time, Neil Simpson hit a low drive from 25 yards that skidded off the surface and over Billy's outstretched arms. Big Billy was not having a good night – and it was to get worse.

We dominated the second half and with about ten minutes to go, Doug Somner equalised with a scrambled effort. The momentum was with us and if any team was to win, it looked more likely to be St Mirren. Then disaster struck. My former team mate, Peter Weir picked up a loose ball and hit a speculative effort. It was not one of the crispest strikes from 'The Sink's' and it looked more likely to stop in the mud before it got to Billy.

As Billy went down to make the standard save, the ball squirmed through his grasp, went through his legs and just managed to cross the line. Game over. Dream over. The dressing room was terrible. Many of the players were in tears, especially Billy Thomson who just sat with his head in his hands, devastated. We had put so much in over the two games, especially the replay, that to go out like that felt cruel. If that was cruel, what was to happen 12 months later was criminal.

In April 1983, we made the semis again and it was back to Parkhead for another crack at glory. This time, it was Rangers who stood in our way. It was a terrible game, in atrocious conditions. I don't know whether we were too anxious because of what happened the previous season, but we simply never turned up and it was no surprise when Sandy Clark opened the scoring for Rangers. In the end we were thankful for a Craig

Paterson own goal in the last few minutes which saw us through to a replay.

Ricky was furious with our non-event of a performance at Parkhead and got us appropriately fired up for the Hampden replay a few days later. This time we ripped into Rangers from the off and dominated the entire 90 minutes, but somehow failed to score, going through enough chances to win several matches.

Extra-time was required and our domination of proceedings continued, but as time wore on, the game got more and more tense. In the 118th minute, a corner to Rangers saw a looping Sandy Clark header easily cleared off the line by Lex. He had been guarding the post and in his knackered state, he was still leaning on the woodwork as he casually blocked the ball. Some of the Rangers players made half-hearted appeals for a goal, but there was no way it came close to crossing the line. Unless your name was Brian McGinlay - perpetually controversial referee from Balfron.

McGinlay – positioned nowhere near enough to have a view of the goal line – blew for a goal. The linesman hadn't even flagged. We were initially stunned and a bit confused. Had he actually awarded a goal? When the reality dawned on us, all Hell broke loose. Once some form of order descended, McGinlay blew for full-time shortly after the restart and now the gloves were really off.

Our sense of injustice and frustration boiled over and McGinlay was surrounded by the entire team, subs and coaching staff. Ricky came into the fray and started to pull us away from McGinlay, who by now was starting to look worried. It was to be no respite, as Ricky was merely wanting the space to make his feelings made personally known to McGinlay.

In the Hampden dressing rooms, the scenes were worse than those at Dens a year earlier. Many tears were shed, but there was also a sense of anger and despair at what had happened.

In any league, the wee teams always seem to have a harder job when playing the big teams in relation to winning decisions from the referee. Quite often this is the difference between a team being perceived as mediocre and a successful side and that evening at Hampden, this point was rammed forcibly down our throats.

Playing against either of the Old Firm during this era in Scottish football this was definitely the case and anyone who says otherwise is deluded, or never actually had the questionable pleasure of experiencing the less than even-handedness of the officials in encounters between provincial clubs and the Glasgow giants.

The chips were down when you played the Old Firm – you were often playing the referee as well and it was very, very hard to break down the barrier of every 50/50 decision going their way. What happened that night was simply sickening for us as pros and God knows how the fans felt. There's always next year was probably on some minds – and they were right.

April 1984 and it was back to Hampden yet again for another semi-final – this time against Celtic. This was during a low point in my career at Love Street as I was at loggerheads with Alex Miller, signing month-to-month deals as I got the increasing feeling that the manager wanted me out of the club.

Despite the clear-the-air talks with some of the senior pros, Alex Miller was systematically eradicating the old guard that in his opinion held too much power within the dressing room at Love Street. Lex had gone to Dundee just prior to the end of Ricky's tenure as manager, closely followed by 'Cowboy' after he fell out with the boss. Make no mistake – I was next on the hit list.

He even went as far as to sign John McGregor on loan from Liverpool and he soon took my first team slot. At least I was to be replaced by a Liverpool player. Alex Miller's plan to eradicate the Rat Pack went spectacularly wrong in the long run. His signings Brian Gallagher, Jim Rooney and Derek Hamilton soon made up the Rat Pack – Part 2 and these guys were way, way out of control compared to what had been in place previously. They definitely brought out the worst in me, so I guess thanks are in order Mr. Miller.

Unfortunately for Alex Miller, I wasn't for shifting even when, as mentioned earlier, a proposed move to Celtic was in the offing in the 1984-85 close season. John McGregor was to get a nasty knee injury when playing for St Mirren - something Saints forgot to tell Liverpool about, who went mental when informed weeks later - and in the cruel world of football, one man's misfortune is another's good fortune. This gave me the opportunity to get back in the team and finally hammer home my worth to the manager. When the chips were down, he knew that he needed me and I took this as a back-handed compliment. Contracts were duly signed and the whole period was put behind us.

Back to the 1984 semi and once more our hopeless quest for silverware came adrift at the last hurdle. This time it wasn't dodgy refereeing, but almost divine intervention from the Man upstairs. As mentioned, I was out of the squad and watched from the Hampden stands, as a massive gale swirled around the famous old ground as the game got underway. At the crucial moments, it was to be the difference between the teams. Brian McClair, deadly finisher as he was, was gifted an opening when a wind assisted through ball shot past our defence and he simply guided it on its speedy way to open the scoring. To the boys' credit, we fought back and were level before half-time when Big Frank McDougall lashed a shot past Pat Bonner.

'Great. It's 1-1 and the wind is behind us in the second half,' I thought optimistically. Wrong. For some strange reason, Miller never set us up to take advantage of the wind in the same way that Celtic did in the opening 45 minutes. Macca was stuck out wide, which nullified his predatory instincts for these conditions and Big Frank was left isolated as ball after ball went shooting around him at warp speed in the mini-hurricane. Celtic never really threatened and most were resigned to the 1-1 scoreline until the weather dealt its fateful blow with only a few minutes left.

Paul McStay had a shot blocked just inside the box and instead of it ballooning over the bar for a corner, the ball seemed to hang in mid-air, its trajectory being altered drastically by the gale and it dropped just over the hopelessly outstretched arms of Billy Thomson as he scrambled backwards to avert the freak effort.

Even sitting in the stands it was a real kick in the guts and I knew instantly that the chance of a Cup Final was gone again – the fourth time in three years. It was soul-destroying.

Downstairs in the dressing room, Big Billy was distraught and our continual calamities in the semi-finals were beginning to turn into some kind of mini-personal disaster for him. The rest of us put it down as a 'weather goal', but the big fella was in a terrible state. Soon afterwards, following a long-running dispute with Miller, Billy was sold to Dundee United. Little was he to know that his experiences of Scottish Cup heartache with St Mirren weren't quite over yet.

In 1985, off we went again like some kind of footballing equivalent of the charge of the Light Brigade in another doomed shot at winning a trophy. The quarter-final saw us drawn at home to Dundee United. A large, noisy crowd packed into Love Street and there was a real edge to the atmosphere, which seemed to work its way on to the pitch.

The teams were closely matched and we really fancied our chances of making it through to the semis, having seen United off at the same stage and venue three years previously. United were a very good team and they were controlling the game with ease, eventually taking the lead. This seemed to finally waken us up and Ian Scanlon slotted a penalty to equalise.

Right - game on, I thought and so did the rest of the boys. United had not taken as much advantage of their superiority and we now had a second chance. The crowd responded and the overall vibe on and off the pitch was -let's get right intae them. United had one soft area of their make up – they could be intimated and put off their stride, if pressure was applied. Our equaliser, the fans going nuts on the terraces and our collective will on the pitch would change the tie in our favour. Or so I thought.

Two minutes after Scan's penalty, Paul Sturrock ran on to a through ball in the St Mirren box. Campbell Money came sliding out to collect and as Sturrock went sliding in, he took him out with a boot right between the eyes. It was a great tackle – one I'd have been proud of, but not in these circumstances.

As the ball went loose and Dibble went into la-la land, 'Luggy' picked himself up and stroked the ball into the net. Amazingly, the ref blew for a goal. Chaos ensued and with a large travelling support helping swell the gate, the roof just about came off the old ground. Just as we had dragged ourselves into the tie and had got our eyes fixed on winning it, this injustice was too much for us, especially combined with the frustrations of the previous few seasons attempts at Cup glory.

The sight of Dibble being stretchered off, blood pouring across his face, plus the realisation that Mark Fulton would have to stand in as keeper, was too much for us. Vengeance was sought.

Shortly after the goal, Stevie Clarke went right through Sturrock. As much as he was a cultured centre-half, Steve was ruthless and as hard as nails. He was quickly surrounded by half the United team and the referee waded in to try and keep the peace.

Sturrock lay prone on the turf just a few yards away, right in front of the St Mirren fans on the Love Street North Bank terracing. I saw my chance. I went up to Sturrock - on the face of it to say 'are you alright, Paul?' – but as the words escaped my lips, I grabbed one of those famous jug ears and slammed his head back off the turf.

Sturrock made an instant recovery, leaping to his feet and throwing a punch which just glanced my left temple – just in time for the ref to witness as he too came to see if Sturrock was OK. Instant red card for 'Luggy' and hee-haw for me, but a sense of justice being done.

Only it wasn't – this was professional football and we had lost the place. You need to keep your focus, no matter what and we lost our composure. United could sense this and despite our one-man advantage, they went on to score twice and ran out comfortable 4-1 winners. This should have been a lesson for us in the importance of keeping our cool. It was a lesson that was not heeded.

If the 1985 quarter final was a testy encounter, then the 1986 quarter final was volcanic. We were drawn to play Hearts, at Tynecastle and we went through to the capital in good spirit, backed by a large and vociferous support. Hearts were a physical team, with plenty of characters and there was a simmering rivalry-cum-bad feeling between the teams that was growing through the repetitive Scottish Premier League schedule of playing each other four times a season. That afternoon, the tension finally boiled over and just like 1985, it was sparked by Dibble being KO'd.

After only ten minutes or so, Dibble was completely taken out by John Colquhoun. The big man was knocked unconscious and being the days of only two subs and these rarely including a keeper, it was clear that we would be playing out the remainder of the game with no recognised goalie.

Neil Cooper went in goals and did his best, but the handicap was too severe and soon the goals began to go in. Our frustration was soon manifesting itself in the form of a toe-to-toe with the Hearts players at every available opportunity. Colquhoun had gone unpunished for his foul on Dibble, yet it was St Mirren who were being punished in reality. The ref was Bob Valentine, who was soon to retire. The events of that afternoon probably speeded up his plans to chuck it – about time too.

ABER'S GONNAE GET YE!

I'd had a run-in with my wife, Anne-Marie the night before and was in a filthy mood to start with. The way our fortunes were flying down the pan once again… well, it was too much for me. The likes of Neil Berry, Kenny Black and Walter Kidd were no shrinking violets and the game soon descended into some form of hand-to-hand combat.

Kenny McDowall and I were certainly leading from the front for the Saints and how we were not sent off I can only put down to the ref feeling guilty about the way things had turned out following his error in the Dibble KO.

Eventually, my chance with Colquhoun came up and I did him good and proper, with one of my 'Man and Ball' specialities, and by 'ball', don't assume it was anything made by Mitre either. He was running onto a through ball, and I accelerated to meet him somewhere close to when he was getting the ball or laying it off. Either way, it was irrelevant. I went through Colquhoun like a freight train, the ball flying one way, him the other, and the Gorgie hordes flying into orbit.

Pre-meditated? You bet, but it felt good. All Hell broke loose and I remember lying on the turf being surrounded by virtually the entire Hearts team, who were threatening me with all sorts.

My reaction of laughter seemed to spook some of them – I think they thought that I had finally lost the plot completely and with my reputation, maybe I was best avoided. We eventually lost 4-1 and the chance of glory had gone again - but we would have the sweetest revenge 12 months later.

As a footnote, St Mirren's relationship with Hearts hit the depths a few weeks later, on the final day of the season when the league title would be decided. Hearts had to avoid defeat at Dundee, while over at Love Street, Celtic had to beat St Mirren by five goals and hope that the Dark Blues would do them a favour at Dens Park. This is exactly what happened, with Celtic ripping us apart and Albert Kidd doing the Heart-breaking on Tayside.

At 2.59pm that day, I am certain that Albert, a stalwart full-back for Dundee, with no great history of goal-scoring, had no idea that he was about to go down in Scottish football folklore. Albert popped up in the 83rd and 89th minutes to score the goals that cost Hearts the league. Never mind what happened at Love Street, all Hearts had to do was avoid defeat, something they came within seven minutes of achieving, but will spend eternity reflecting on why they didn't.

We got slaughtered in sections of the media, who were hinting that St Mirren had laid down to Celtic, in particular, ex-Celts Frank McGarvey and Peter Mackie. I can categorically assure you dear reader, that these claims are complete bollocks, to use a technical term.

Admittedly, Mackie's miss of an open goal from four yards with the score at 0-0 doesn't look clever in the context of the argument, but this sort of miss was not uncommon from Peter. The guy who got the biggest slating was Frank McGarvey, who had rejoined St Mirren from Celtic only 12 months previously. Despite Frank's views to the contrary, we were not a one-man team, so he cannot be accused of single-handedly throwing the game.

What caused the problems for Frank was that he was seen congratulating his ex-colleagues after the full-time whistle. With hindsight, this wasn't such a clever thing to do, especially in front of the cameras and it gave the ammunition to those aggrieved at what had happened.

The suggestions that we laid down were an insult to us as people, never mind our professional credibility. Celtic were a better team than St Mirren. They had to try and score as many as they could, while we had nothing to play for. Consequently, we were simply blown away. It was not one of our best performances, but not one of the worst either. This was little comfort to the devastated Jambos, but their St Mirren nightmare was soon to get much, much worse.

8 Once... Twice... Three Times A Red Card

SEASON 1986-1987 began in fairly nondescript style, as we got off to a slow start and we were soon in mid-table. The Rat Pack of Gallagher, Hamilton and Abercromby was still in full swing, with young starlets of the Fergie's Furies team Tony Fitzpatrick, Frank McGarvey and myself, now being the senior pros.

Frank was still in his own wee platform in the dressing room, never short of an opinion and still in possession of awesome self-belief. Tony was - and still is - every inch the decent, upstanding member of the community. He probably even went to confession to plead for forgiveness for the sins of the Rat Pack. I was now team captain – proof that the lunatics can sometimes take over the asylum.

Talented left-winger, Ian Cameron was now a first team-regular, despite his tender years and was in competition for that spot with Gardner Speirs. Gardner had started to pick up some bad injuries, which ultimately curtailed a very promising career, but Ian was a more than able replacement and definitely a member of my Left Peg Culture Club with his greatest strength being the way he seemed to have the ball "superglued" to his left foot as took off on mesmerising dribbles down the wing.

Ian was a bright lad, nicknamed 'The Professor' as he was at Glasgow University doing an accountancy degree. He was a warm, decent, intelligent human being. As he looked across the dressing room at the Rat Pack each day, I shudder to think what he thought of us. Brian Gallagher was certifiable and Derek 'Deeksy' Hamilton and myself were probably starting to push the disciplinary boundaries in regards to our boozing habits. We made up for it by being fanatical trainers, but we may not have been setting the best example to the younger players. Fortunately, Ian had the brains to see us as a warning, not an inspiration.

The other two outstanding young talents that we had on the verge of being first team regulars were two local lads - Brian Hamilton and Paul Lambert. Brian was named 'Max Headroom' on account of his flat top hairstyle and was an easy-going lad, who joined in with a lot of the dressing room flak that regularly flew around. On the pitch, he was a great passer of the ball and extremely composed. Never flustered, his range of passing was a great compliment to the midfield engine room veterans of Tony and myself.

Paul Lambert was an outstanding young player. Unfortunately for him, he was my boot room boy and I would give him a real hard time. He was a really skinny wee boy, and Derek Hamilton always claimed that Paul had to run around in the shower to get wet. This is all part and parcel of life at a pro club, where the young lads get a Hell of a runaround from the older pros and I guess my treatment of Paul was all part of a learning curve. That curve, of course, was ultimately to end with him being a European Champions League winner with Borussia Dortmund, winning everything in sight with Celtic and being captain of Scotland.

Having my boots thrown back at him for not being clean enough was probably not the greatest start to his career. Seriously though, Paul was a great listener, even then and you could see that he was willing to learn whatever he could from the likes of Tony, Frank, myself and the other senior pros. As a consequence, despite his lack of physical attributes compared to opposition players he was more than capable of being a great first team player, even at the tender age of 17.

Another young midfielder was signed - probably to help the creaking bones of Fitzpatrick and Abercromby - and what a significant player he was to be for St Mirren. Ian Ferguson arrived from Clyde early on in the season and immediately made an impact on colleagues and supporters. He looked just like a young Dalglish and he played like 'The King' as well. He had massive determination, self-confidence and strong-mindedness – characteristics that were evident on AND off the pitch.

To be honest, Dibble, Tony, Gal, Deeksy and myself were of the opinion that he was an arrogant wee bastard and he let everyone in turn know what his opinion was of them, which won our respect. He was intimidated by nobody – probably a trait he picked up from his upbringing as a die-hard Rangers fan living on Janefield Street in the shadow of Parkhead. The

ABER'S GONNAE GET YE!

great thing about Fergie was that he never knew when to shut up, despite having the reputation of not being favourite to win Mastermind. To that end, he was quickly christened 'BOB', which stood for Brain Of Britain.

On Wednesday October 29th, we had a midweek league game at Love Street against Motherwell. All fairly mundane stuff, but little was I to realise that this was to be the night that my career would change forever. As the game wore on, Gardner Speirs went past a couple of players down the left wing and surged into the box only to be brought down. The ref, Louis Thow pointed to the penalty spot and went running to the bye-line.

Motherwell's Stevie Kirk grabbed the ball as he was a wee bit peeved at the decision to award us a penalty. Actually, he was severely p****d off. I went to grab the ball off him and we had a wee tussle – handbags I think is the technical term. As we squared up, Kirk gave me the 'Glasgow Kiss' and down I went from the headbutt. Now I know that Thow didn't actually see the incident and as he galloped across in Kirk's direction and quickly flashed a straight red at him, I began to think that something was amiss here.

As Stevie marched off the pitch, Thow turned his attention to me: 'The two of you were at it.' he barked and quickly flourished a red card at me. I knew and so did he that he didn't see the incident, yet he was giving me a red card for something he never saw. I lost it:

'You are nothing but a f*****g b*****d,' I yelled at him.

Then I said it again. This time even louder.

Red card No. 2 was waved at me. Bedlam had broken out and our coaching staff, plus a couple of Strathclyde Police's finest were now on the pitch. Thow was being jostled by Saints players and coaching staff, each one incensed by what they were seeing. I got to about five yards from the touchline, when I could hear Ian Ferguson yelling: 'Don't walk off Aber, the ref wants another word – you'll only make it worse.'

He ran over and grabbed me and as I shouted at Fergie: 'Get tae f**k,' the stupid sod managed to swing me round so that I delivered this latest piece of Tourette's Syndrome patter directly at the onrushing Thow. Cheers Fergie! Thow just about exploded. A perfect match for his by now beetroot coloured coupon, red card No. 3 was duly issued.

'You're still a f*****g b*****d!' was my parting shot at the ref as I was shoved up the tunnel to the dressing room by coaching staff and Police.

Afterwards in the dressing room, everything was remarkably calm. I thought that the three cards had counted only as one sending off and that Thow had only kept waving them around as he was having a temper tantrum and was trying to make his point.

How many F's and B's did he want? Would he have stopped at six cards? I was in the wrong, but to a degree, so was Thow. He had clearly lost the place and was having a refereeing nervous breakdown. I had seen many players get a red card and give the ref a piece of their mind as they went off. The worst that happened was that the ref told them to 'beat it' – or words to that effect. That night was no different, yet somehow I had ended up going toe-to-toe with a guy showing more cards than a Vegas croupier.

After the final whistle, the 1-0 win for Saints seemed irrelevant as confusion began to reign in the dressing-room as conflicting verdicts of what fate awaited me flew around the room from my colleagues. I was still of the view that it was only one red card waved repeatedly in a fit of rage, but something was niggling at me that all was not what I thought it to be.

I asked the gaffer, Alex Miller, who was very calm about the whole thing: 'Boss, what did the other two cards mean?' He didn't know, but popped round to the ref's room just to see what was the final outcome. He was away a while and I began to feel now that something definitely wasn't right.

Eventually, Alex came back in looking ashen-faced - even more so than normal. 'Billy, I'm going to have to verify what this means,' he said. 'This is completely unheard of….' and his voice trailed off. Thow had shown me three straight red cards in one game. Never mind s**t creek, I was in excrement estuary and never mind the paddle, I didn't even have a canoe.

I managed to slope away from the ground without too much hassle from the Press - it wasn't exactly a fixture that had the journalists flocking - but the next day there were plenty of reporters awaiting my arrival at the ground. 'No comment' was my official line, but this was no cliché. I didn't know what to say. The case was to go to the SFA and we would soon hear the outcome.

In the meantime, it was being suggested that there was a fair chance that I would be banned sine die – a lifetime ban. My career would be finished. It was achieving interest on a national scale and that Saturday's Football Focus on BBC 1 saw Bob Wilson holding his own inquest into events. I was being held up as the worst example of the growing problem within football of dissent to refs. The irony of this was that dissent was not one of my usual offences, yet here I was being held up as an example to British football as to what was wrong with the modern game.

The rumours of a life ban began to get stronger and despite outward appearances of a casual approach, I was in bits. All I had ever wanted to be was a professional footballer and it looked like it was about to be cut short in my late 20s – not by injury, but by the disciplinary panel at the SFA, to whom I wasn't exactly a stranger. The consensus was that Billy Abercromby had been sailing close to the disciplinary code for years and this was the time for his comeuppance. I was very, very worried about my future. My whole life's dreams and ambitions were about to be taken from me and I was powerless to do anything about it. I had never felt so alone.

Eventually, the judgement was passed and I was given a then British all-comers record – a 12 match ban. I was relieved as it could have been much worse, but everyone else seemed to be gasping at the length of the ban.

To me, it wasn't a big problem. I had served four and five match bans in the past as a consequence of the totting-up procedure and injuries could see a player out for much longer than 12 matches.

The length of the ban was supposed to be used as an example to others. An example of what? Did anyone see a reduction in dissent towards officials? No. The whole thing was blown out of all proportion, right from the minute when Thow started chasing me across the Love Street turf, blowing his whistle like a demented polis and waving card after card at me. Three swear words resulted in a 12-game ban. What would the punishment have been if I had really opened up on him? What if Thow hadn't stopped at three. It was ridiculous.

The esteemed St Mirren board of directors and manager Alex Miller had some ideas of their own. Following an emergency meeting after the announcement of the ban, I was summoned to see the manager. He informed me that I would be fined the maximum two weeks' wages, would be stripped of the captaincy and most damning of all, I was being placed on the transfer list.

'Nothing to do with the ban,' said Miller to the Press. 'Just a chance for Billy to get a fresh start elsewhere.' What absolute nonsense.

Just as had happened to Jim Clunie, it is my belief that the directors didn't want St Mirren to be associated with a now-notorious player. Rather than try and support me through the period and recognise my then ten years-plus at the club, they chose to try and shunt me out of Love Street. I think they felt that they had to be seen to act, in addition to the SFA punishment.

I was raging. There was no way these people were going to force me out of the club that had become such a massive part of my life. As it happens, no serious bids came in for me, as I was widely considered damaged goods as a result of the furore surrounding the incident. And anyway, I couldn't even play reserve football to keep up match fitness and sharpness, so I was no use to anyone.

Nonetheless, the knives were out for me at the place I had come to think of as my second home. The fact the manager wanted shot of me was no great surprise and this was the perfect opportunity. The knowledge that the board of directors thought so little of me simply made me feel increasingly angry and determined - there was no way these people would drive me out.

9 Broke, Busted And Disgusted... Guess Who's Back?

I SAT in the stands and watched every single one of the 12 games that I was banned from attending on the pitch. That's a lot of time to ponder your next move, I can assure you. Banned by the SFA. Fined by St Mirren. Stripped of the captaincy and placed on the transfer list.

I was now portrayed as some kind of football outlaw and there were more than a few in the game and the Press who were delighted to see this. Early on, I made my mind up. I was going to come back – faster, stronger, fitter and even more unrepentant than ever before. The SFA, Alex Miller, the directors – I was going to show them that you don't mess with Billy Abercromby. The end result would be beyond my wildest dreams.

My team-mates were great and I was the subject of some really cutting dressing room humour that I took in the spirit in which it was meant. I would have been the first to dish it out, so I had no choice but to take it. I even joined in by having my photo taken at Love Street by the Daily Record, with me sitting on one of 12 footballs all lined up in a row to mark out the record ban. My presence at the club was creating an uncomfortable atmosphere with the management and directors, but unfortunately for them I was beginning to revel in this. The players could see a mile off what was going on and to a man they backed me to make a comeback.

I set about not just keeping fit, but by using the period of suspension - I couldn't even play reserve football - to get as fit as I had been in my life. I was being put through a pre-season workout, but instead of three weeks, this was being extended over 12 weeks. Quickly, I probably became the fittest player at the club, if not in Scotland. I guess the SFA had done me a favour. I would be ready to play again as soon as the suspension had been served. This was my sole focus. Mentally it was tough, training as hard as possible, in the full knowledge that there was no possibility of first team action at the end of it. My burning desire to return with a bang was what kept me going. Soon, I was to get an unexpected boost.

In December, Alex Miller resigned to take over at Hibernian. I had seen him off and this gave me a huge morale boost. St Mirren moved quickly to get a new managerial team in place and it was to be a great move for all at the club. Stirling Albion manager, Alex Smith was to be the new St Mirren boss and his assistant was my old friend and colleague Jimmy Bone. My nightmare was over.

Alex was massively respected within the game and was the SFA Staff Coach at their highly regarded Largs HQ. His knowledge of the game was second to none and his contacts were endless. He seemed to immediately take a liking to me, despite my non-availability as a player. The feeling was mutual. He was a smashing guy, very laid back, even in a crisis. He was also a smart thinker and was able to get key points across to the players without ever having to raise his voice – people listened when he spoke, it was as simple as that.

Not long after taking over, Alex had got wind that despite my ferocious training, I was probably not being quite as professional as I should be in regard to my 'refuelling' sessions of an evening. I was called into his office and he let me speak. He let me waffle on for ages with a series of convoluted excuses for my behaviour.

'Billy, I think you are being economical with the truth, son,' he said as I ended my adults' only version of Jackanory.

'What do you mean boss?'

'What I mean is that you are a lying wee b*****d!'

And with that he smiled, gave me a wink and ushered me out of his office. Respect was mutual and I was probably closer to him than most of the other players. He let me away with murder and I make no excuses for giving him the nickname 'Faither'.

Having 'Papa' Bone as his No.2 was great for Tony, Frank, Dibble and myself, who had all been former playing comrades. There was a mutual understanding and he knew exactly how to handle the players, giving - literally - kicks up the backside where required and geeing up the more sensitive ones when they needed it most. Jimmy's version of man-management regarding my own position - I was still stripped of the captaincy and on the transfer list - was a masterclass.

One morning at training, as we set off on a few laps of the pitch, Jimmy started running beside me. As we finished Lap 1, he said: 'You're off the transfer list, Aber.' I was ecstatic. We kept jogging along and as we finished Lap 2, he said: 'Alright skipper?' And as if my joy couldn't increase more, he said at the end of Lap 3: 'There are two weeks wages waiting for you at reception.'

Not only was I off the transfer list, re-instated as team captain, despite having several games still to serve on the ban, Jimmy and Alex had managed to get my two weeks' wages back. Talk about installing self-belief in a player. I would have run through a brick wall, or Neil Berry and Kenny Black, for Smith and Bone as a result of their faith in me.

In retrospect, it was a smart move, as it was a young squad and although Alex was a master at organising a team, he still needed his leaders out on the pitch. I was to be one of these and he now had my unfaltering loyalty.

The other marvellous thing that Alex and Jimmy brought to Love Street was their re-working of the club's internal disciplinary code. Instead of handing out fines for petty offences such as being late for training, Alex and Jimmy introduced a forfeit style code where the guilty parties would have to get up on the physio's table in the home dressing room, each Monday morning, to perform a story/joke/song to the rest of the squad.

Quickly, these events gained in notoriety and Love Street effectively closed for their duration as ground staff, players, coaching staff and secretaries all piled into the dressing room to see the latest star turn.

The idea was that the offenders would be humiliated into never ever wanting to repeat their misdemeanours. In the case of a visibly shaking Paul Lambert, skipping ropes acting as a microphone and struggling with the lyrics to Baa, Baa, Black Sheep - his choice of track it has to be said - then the object of the exercise was achieved. Although Paul was probably psychologically scarred for life by the experience.

However, there were that many nutcases in the dressing room that the whole plan backfired as more and more players were committing small disciplinary infringements, so that they could get their big chance on the stage/table. Derek Hamilton's lateness for training increased during this period, as part of a deliberate ploy on his part to develop his burgeoning career as a rock singer. In his own mind at least. It was like Stars in Your Eyes gone horribly wrong.

'Well Derek, who are you going to be today?'

'Tonight Jimmy, I'm going be Rod Stewaaaart!' (Again).

'Do do do dooooo doooo…….do You Think I'm Sexy?'

'No!

The main difference to Stars in their Eyes was that on TV, the worst case scenario was that Matthew Kelly would commiserate with you not winning and it would be back to performing in clubland.

In the Love Street dressing room any performers who failed to cut it with the critics would be dragged into the shower area, where 19-year-old man child, Ian Ferguson would be waiting as executioner and turn a fire hose on the victim. Fergie seemed to enjoy this to a worrying degree and bearing in mind he had only been at the club a matter of months - his self-confidence was astounding.

Whilst Elvis may not have left the building at the end of another of Deeksy's star turns, it was Steve Clarke's turn to exit stage left during January 1987. Steve had been getting well-deserved recognition for some time and from the start of the season, a number of suitors seemed to be keeping a very close eye on his situation, which was further enhanced by his deteriorating relationship with Alex Miller.

By the time Smith and Bone took over, it was just a matter of when, rather than if, Stevie would move on, but this never affected his performances and commitment to the cause, which probably speaks volumes about his mental strength.

I don't think that there was any problem with Stevie and the new management team, but by the turn of the year it was simply a case of St Mirren and Stevie agreeing on a sale that suited both parties - a big fee for the club and a good career move for the player. In the pre-Bosman days, this was about as good a situation as you could hope for in the circumstances and everyone was happy when Chelsea finally agreed a fee of £400,000. What happened for Stevie's career over the coming years was simply magical, with a long and successful playing career that ended some years later, still a Chelsea player, winning plenty of silverware along the way.

His lack of Scotland caps was truly mystifying – maybe that St Mirren association couldn't be shaken off. Since finishing playing he has gone on to be a highly-respected coach, working with some of the managerial greats of the game – including his adversary from Paisley and Rotterdam in the early 80s – Ruud Gullit. I wonder if Ruud ever held up the performances of Stevie and Phil McAveety in Rotterdam as an example of defending away from home in Europe.

Meanwhile, I was still turning up for training every day, safe in the knowledge that I had no chance of any competitive action as a consequence of my lengthy ban. However, I knew that once the suspension was up, Alex and Jimmy wanted me straight back in the first team.

Fitzy had suffered a badly broken jaw earlier in the season and the young midfield was badly in need of an old head. I had been used to shorter bans in the past, so maintaining some form of training discipline was nothing new, but this was different. I had been written off by everyone, including certain journalists who had been gagging for me to get a lifetime ban. Now I could see that I would be back and I wanted to come back stronger than ever. In addition, I would be available for the crucial second half of the season, fresher than anyone else in the team and more importantly, the opposition. I guess I owed Louis Thow a big thank you - aye, right.

I made my comeback in January 1987, just in time for our annual tilt at the Scottish Cup. In the Third Round tie, we were drawn at home to Inverness Caledonian of the Highland League. This was no walkover and the 3-0 scoreline flattered us, although Fergie's final goal, a free-kick from easily 35 yards, was good enough to win any game. The other goals were scored by Kenny McDowall and Frank McGarvey, but Inverness could quite easily have won the game.

We were relieved to be through and when we got to the dressing room, there was an unexpected boost. Graeme Souness was in his first season at Rangers and they were sweeping all before them, already having the League Cup in the Ibrox trophy room and the league title was looking likely. They were cast iron favourites to win the Scottish Cup, but news began to filter through that a few miles down the road, Hamilton Accies had just beaten Rangers 1-0 at Ibrox. As soon as we heard the news, the old heads of McGarvey, Fitzpatrick and Abercromby began to think that this could be our year.

The next round saw us drawn away at Renfrewshire rivals Morton. The old ground was packed out and despite the incessant rain, the atmosphere was white hot, on and off the pitch. We were rubbish, but somehow managed to get out of jail. Morton had two old Love Street faces in their team, Rowan Alexander and more significantly, my old pal Lex Richardson. They were desperate to beat us and to be honest, they probably should have.

The turning point happened straight after Morton went 2-1 up in the second half. Footballing wisdom decrees that the most likely time for a team to concede a goal is straight after scoring one themselves, which is precisely what happened.

Straight from the kick off, Moon Man went on a charge that took him flying into the Morton box at full speed. God knows what he was going to do with the ball, but this was soon irrelevant, as he was brought down for a penalty. To show how garbage we were, Fergie – usually deadly – needed to knock in the rebound, failing to score first time.

With Morton's advantage quickly nullified, the momentum was finally with St Mirren and with five minutes to go, Paul Chalmers latched on to a great lofted through ball from Kenny and somehow managed to shrug off a strong challenge from Davie Wylie in the Morton goal and tuck the loose ball in from a tight angle. It was great finish on a treacherous surface and the huge travelling St Mirren support went suitably mental. Afterwards, the feeling was spreading that this could be our year after all.

Next up was the quarter-final. We were drawn away to Raith Rovers and some form of cup fever was beginning to grip Paisley. As we warmed-up on the park there were Saints fans in all corners of the ground and we were informed in the dressing-room that the kick-off would be delayed to allow the fans to get in.

Tension was rising during the wait, especially among the younger lads and that was when the experienced players such as Frank and myself came into our own, cracking jokes and keeping the mood focused and positive.

It must have worked as Big Basil put us 1-0 up quite early on and we were looking comfortable. However, we couldn't find that crucial killer second goal and as time wore on, we found ourselves fighting a defensive rearguard against the Fife side. In the last minute, Paul Chalmers did it again with a nice cool finish to see us through to yet another semi-final. Now the feeling was unanimous – this WAS going to be our year.

The draw for the semi-final saw us meet Hearts, at Hampden Park. The previous year's debacle at Tynecastle still rankled and there was further bad blood as many of the Hearts support seemed to harbour the misguided view that St Mirren had laid down to Celtic at the dramatic climax of their ill-fated attempt to win the league that year. The league matches in 1986-87 between the sides had been bad-tempered affairs to put it mildly and we were all fired-up to see them off at Hampden.

In the build-up for the game, Alex Smith showed his true mettle as a great thinker about the game. We were safe in the league and it really was a case of throwing the kitchen sink at winning the Scottish Cup.

Alex persuaded the directors to pay for the squad to spend a few days at the start of the week leading up to the semi-final at Seamill Hydro, on the Ayrshire coast. This was a tactic often used by Celtic before their big games and Alex was sending out the message that this was a special game for us. Down the coast, we spent the early part of the week doing some training and working on specific tactical ploys for the game. A few beers were had as well, just to calm the nerves, but nobody abused the relaxed rules – a minor miracle given some of the personnel involved.

Dave Winnie had been having terrible injury problems all season and his place in the semi was in jeopardy. I think some of the other centre-halves were injured as well, because Alex took me to one side and said: 'Aber – d'you fancy playing sweeper on Saturday?' He put no pressure on me, knowing full well that I had never played in that position before, but I said that if that was required for the good of the team, then: 'Aye – no worries Boss.' Fortunately, Dave passed his fitness test and the Abercromby Sweeper Experiment never came to light.

We went back to our families for a couple of days relaxation and then it was off to Hampden. In the dressing room, Frank was banging on about how Hearts had a few key players out suspended – particularly lethal striker, John Robertson – but they would be back if there was a replay. In Frank's humble opinion, we would have to win it at the first time of asking and that would be no problem.

Fitzy was still injured, but he was still delivering his unstinting positivity to the younger players and as we got ready to go out, there was no doubt in my mind that this time we would win a semi. As we ran out, the players were immediately met by a mass of St Mirren fans in Hampden's traditional Rangers End. This was the only part of the ground terracing with a roof and although the 15,000 Saints fans were outnumbered by The Jambos, they were easily winning the battle of noise. What a lift this gave us players and we soon started to dominate proceedings.

Eventually, Fergie gave us a first half lead when he rounded Henry Smith away out on the far edge of the box and calmly slotted home from a very acute angle in front of the delirious Buddies. It was a great finish and another mark of Ian's growing reputation as one of the hottest properties in Scottish football.

We continued to dominate proceedings, but got a sickener when Gary McKay steered a curling effort past Dibble and in off the upright for Hearts to equalise against the run of play. Now, at this point we could have wobbled and gone to pieces, but crucially we didn't. The players encouraged each other and with immediate determination we took the fight back to Hearts.

With about seven minutes to go a ball slowly floated over Frank McGarvey's head in the Hearts' box. With his back to goal, Frank swivels round, hits the ball on the half volley to send it past Henry Smith and into the corner of the net. Bedlam.

Only Frank could score a goal like that – there looked to be nothing on, but with his vast experience, skill and poacher's instinct, he had come up trumps big time. Strangely, while all around us there was chaos, on the pitch we kept the head and saw out the remaining minutes quite safely.

When the final whistle went, my immediate emotion was a combination of elation and relief. At last. After the heartbreak of the previous five years, we had made it to a major final.

The feelings were shared with the support, who had been through the mill with the players during the same period. St Mirren had last won the Cup in 1959 and the achievement of even reaching the final was massive. Purely on a career basis, this was a major achievement, but at a club as small as St Mirren, moments like that were few and far between and the sense of shared delight amongst players, staff and fans was tangible.

I can clearly remember looking round to see Brian Gallagher, who was out with a long-term injury, hirpling across the turf in a particularly tasteless beige suit, with a smile as wide as the Clyde. You'd have though that he had scored the winner himself and that kind of summed up the camaraderie among the players. As we stood in front of the celebrating masses behind the goals, you couldn't help but think we ARE going win this bloody thing.

Dundee United were victorious in the other semi and while they spent the interim period between then and the May final going on a charge through some of the greats of European football such as Barcelona en route to the UEFA Cup Final - a genuinely magnificent achievement - we were in a strange limbo land. League safety was assured, but we wouldn't be finishing in the European qualifying slots. As a result, players could be rested and others could be given a chance to get fit before the big day.

In one game at Aberdeen, Willie 'I am the Ref' Miller managed to get himself sent off and on his way to the dressing rooms - which took a while, as the bold Willie was initially refusing to walk, such was his shock that someone had actually dared show him the red card - he passed me.

I was laughing at the whole thing, which made Willie even angrier. He just started shouting utter gibberish at me, stuff to do with the 12-game ban was about all I could make out, but this made me almost double over in hysterics: 'F*****g b*****d Abercromby… life ban ya b*****d… 12 games… f**k…..' on an on he went. I decided to wave him a big bye-bye and pointed to the tunnel. At this point Willie needed to be restrained and it was pointed out to me afterwards that if he had got to me, I might have missed the final due to me being hospitalised in Aberdeen.

On a more serious point, it was then highlighted that I was one booking away from a three-match ban and that would mean missing the final. If Willie Miller could get sent off, then nothing was impossible – I was going to have to be careful. Alex and Jimmy decided to rest me for a couple of games because of this.

The last day of the league season saw us visit Ibrox on the occasion of them being crowned Premier League champions for the first time in years – the crowning glory on the first season of The Souness Revolution. There was a full-house at Ibrox, making a Hell of a din as you could imagine and Alex and Jimmy thought that this would be the perfect warm-up for the following week's Cup Final, especially for some of the younger players.

After months on the sidelines with injury, Tony Fitzpatrick made his return to the team in a desperate bid to prove his fitness ahead of the biggest game of his career. It must have been agony for Tony – he was such a massive part of the club and his old long-time colleagues McGarvey and Abercromby would be playing. It would have been so cruel if he had missed out after all his years service to St Mirren.

Paul Lambert made way for him and I could sense that Paul was panic-stricken. Was he going to miss out due to Tony's return? Alex had a wee word with Paul and all seemed well – it was soon apparent that the boy wonder from Linwood would be starting the final, at the age of 17, whilst

ABER'S GONNAE GET YE!

Fitzy was playing to try and guarantee a subs slot.

As for myself, all I had to do was keep out of trouble for 90 minutes and I knew that I would be leading the team out on that historic occasion. Easy, or so I thought.

A couple of month previously, we'd had a tousy encounter with Rangers at Love Street. At some point, I had gone in late on Ian Durrant – just to let him know I was there as the pros put it. Souness, who was playing that day, took grave exception to this and decided to try to sort me out as vengeance for this perceived attack on his young star midfielder.

For the next 20 or 30 minutes, we launched into a series of fully committed challenges on each other, with neither coming out on top. Eventually, the slug fest came to a close when Souness subbed himself. But as he began to trot off, he span round, pointed at me and said: 'I'll f*****g see you at Ibrox Abercromby.'

I burst out laughing and casually waved him off – which probably didn't help. The game he was promising to see me at - and I think we all know what Graeme was meaning - was that final league match where I had to stay out of harm's way and the ref's notebook.

Alex had a word with referee Kenny Hope - who by chance would also be the Cup Final ref - along the lines of: 'Any problems with Aber – tip me the nod and I'll sub him.' That was one problem solved, now what was that about harm's way? Souness wasn't playing – surely there would be no problem on that score?

A few minutes into the game and I had just finished hitting a long crossfield pass when I could see Graeme Roberts careering across the Ibrox turf, like a heavyweight Exocet and I was the target. I just cleared his desperate lunge in time. Fair enough, I thought, Robbo's just a bit pumped up for the occasion.

Five minutes later, in he came again. Whoosh! I just got out of the way of another potential amputation below the knee. "F**k's sake Robbo!" I shouted. He just winked, smiled and then never went near me again. All very strange.

Whether this had anything to do with my previous encounter with Graeme Souness, I'll never know. But if he's still a bit upset about that game at Love Street, I'm more than happy to meet up with him to chat about it over a cup of tea and a bun. Any time, big man – any time.

So that was that then. Rangers won the game 1-0 to lift the league title, but all that mattered now was focusing on May 16th 1987 and ensuring that it was to be an era and career-defining afternoon. Little was I to know as we left Ibrox at 5.30pm, with 40,000 Rangers fans still inside going bananas - or is that oranges - that my plan for a quiet build-up was going to go ever so slightly wrong.

10 The Greatest Day

STRAIGHT after the Rangers game, phone calls to Love Street from the media started to vary from the Cup Final build-up. Relations between my wife, Anne-Marie and myself had been going downhill fast and it's fair to say that things weren't working out. I had moved out of our Lochwinnoch house and bought a house in Kilbarchan. Anne-Marie was also expecting our second daughter, Hayley and by the time of her birth on September 3rd 1987, the marriage was effectively over, in acrimonious circumstances. It's something that I am certainly not proud of, but it was hardly a unique tale of a marriage break-up. She went on to be a fabulous mother to the girls, but I will touch on this later.

In the week leading up to the Final, Anne-Marie had gone to the papers to give her side of the story and the papers focused on tales of me being too drunk to shave in the morning, let alone make training and other such juicy tales that the tabloids love.

Normally, this may have only got a few column inches near the front of the tabloids, but the timing of the story altered all of this. Alex and Jimmy had repeated the build-up to the semi and had booked Seamill for the first three days of the week. The idea was to get all the boys away from the media build-up and focus on the Final in a relaxed environment. My domestic situation was to put these plans to the test.

On the Monday morning at Love Street there were several journalists waiting for me asking my views on the story, which would break the following day. I just put my head down and set about getting home to Lochwinnoch to pick up a few things before heading to Seamill. Jimmy Bone said that he would handle things in the press and just told me to concentrate on the game.

When I arrived at Lochwinnoch, I found another pack of journalists camped outside my house. This was starting to get silly, but again I kept my mouth shut.

When I got to Seamill, the place was soon crawling with the same journalists from Love Street and Lochwinnoch. While being reasonably sympathetic to my situation, it was clear that Alex and Jimmy's patience was being tested. Alex called me over in the foyer: 'Aber – get rid of them - now.'

I wandered outside to meet the Press, not exactly in the way that I had envisaged as captain of the cup finalists in the week of the game. I told them: 'OK boys, just print what you are going to print. I have no further comment.'

But off the record, I explained the disruption that was being felt by the St Mirren management and the Press guys understood this and left shortly afterwards. They probably didn't want any problems getting access to the St Mirren players in the run-up to the final.

The training preparations got underway and I put all my troubles firmly to the back of my mind. The mood in the camp was extremely upbeat and the camaraderie of the boys was coming to the fore. We really felt that our name was on the cup – provided we did the job to the best of our abilities.

What also caused a lot of merriment was that we had recorded a Cup Final song - what else but When the Saints Go Marching In, with new lyrics relating to the final at Hampden. The song was murdered by the players and staff and the recording session was hysterical.

'Moon Man's' long awaited debut on vinyl must have caused him to suffer stage fright, as his message to the fans over the backing track of the song on the B-side was barely coherent. I think the liquid relaxants may have had something to do with that, as well as being the reason why Brian Gallagher sounded unsure of his own name: 'Hello – I'm errrr Brian Gallagher...' The Beatles at Abbey Road it certainly wasn't.

Booze couldn't be blamed for the worst line of the players' messages on the B-side. That belonged to a 17-year old Paul Lambert: 'Be there or be square!' piped the teenage wonderkid - something that will haunt him to the end of his days any time it is played back to him.

However, since starting to write this book I have discovered the real culprit is my publisher, Norman Macdonald, who made up that 'Be there or be square' line when Paul was in the recording booth, struggling to think of something to say in his message. You have a lot to answer for, Mr Macdonald.

Coming down for breakfast fashionably late on the Tuesday morning, with room-mate 'Moon Man' at my side, we were greeted with the sight of the entire squad and staff sitting holding up newspapers in front of themselves. 'My Cup Final Hubby Was a Drunken Heel' were the front pages of The Sun and the Daily Record not too far behind either with 'Bad Boy Billy'. Then laughter erupted around the room – there was no way my team-mates were going to let me off with this one, but being amongst that cocoon of dressing-room banter was probably the best place to be at that time and there was no way they would let my predicament get to me.

Anne-Marie had understandably really put the boot in and the pages were full of colourful tales and allegations. Then Jimmy Bone's quotes appeared as the case for the defence. Jimmy had been a tad economical with the truth, describing me as a 'fit young man... an athlete in prime condition... and a great example to his team-mates'. As this was read out, the place was rocking with laughter. Perhaps the whole episode had helped reduce tension in the squad – for my colleagues I was certainly proving a hilarious diversion from the big game ahead.

The training at Seamill went well and then it was back to Paisley on Thursday for a couple of light sessions at Love Street and a night back with the families. Obviously, this was a non-starter for yours truly, so I decided to spend Thursday night in a Glasgow hotel, where I spent the night alone watching TV, almost basking in the brief period of quiet anonymity. To try and guarantee a low profile, when the girl on the reception desk asked what my name was, I managed to check in under the following alias: 'The name's Bone. James Bone.' Not exactly Sir Sean Connery, but I though that Jimmy Bone would appreciate the thought.

There was also to be another special change of plan from Smith and Bone. The players and staff were to stay at the Excelsior Hotel, at Glasgow Airport on the Friday night. It was a great idea and it went a long way to helping further bond the team and settle the nerves. Alex announced the team at a meeting in one of the function suites that evening, although by that stage most of us had figured the line-up.

I knew I was playing, but the only real question was over Tony - would he miss out on the biggest game of his career? He was named as a sub and was suitably delighted, with Paul Lambert starting in midfield. One interesting wee problem was that Ian 'The Professor' Cameron was named as the other sub. Ian wasn't there to hear the news either, but for all the right reasons.

ABER'S GONNAE GET YE!

Unbelievably, his accountancy degree exams were on the morning of the final, so a night at the Excelsior with the 'Rat Pack' was hardly ideal preparation. So, off he went home to do some last-minute revising – it probably helped keep his mind off the final. Ian turned up at the hotel at 11.45am on the Saturday, as agreed, with a big smile on his face. He was sure he had passed - I told you that confidence was surging through the squad. We were all delighted to see him and his arrival seemed to signal that it was finally all systems go.

A police escort accompanied the team bus on the journey to Hampden and on the way we could see more and more people decked out in St Mirren's black and white colours heading the same way – all with huge smiles. The feel good factor was spreading. I was quite relaxed on the journey and just wanted to take the whole day in. Some of the younger lads were a bit hyper probably not helped by Ian Ferguson doling out a massive bag of wine gums. There is no truth in the rumour that Derek Hamilton was trying to liquidise them.

Once inside the Hampden dressing room, the mood began to quieten. It was time to deliver. Everyone was out on the pitch doing their warm-up and I found myself alone in the huge dressing room with Alex Smith.

'Are you no' going out Aber?' he asked.

'Aye, boss - just want to finish this cup of tea.'

Alex smiled, recognising that my usual relaxed persona was still in place.

'Are you going to do it for me Aber?'

'Aye, no problem, Faither.'

And that was it – the end of a one-on-one team talk between the manager and captain of the cup finalists, 25 minutes before kick-off. I'll never ever forget it. It was a special moment for me and I hope it was for Alex as well.

As I ran onto the pitch for my brief warm-up, the first thing that hit me was the size of the crowd. Many media sceptics had been saying that with a final not involving either half of the Old Firm for the first time in years, the ground would be less than half-full. Wrong. Back then Hampden was a huge bowl of terracing, with only the Main Stand containing seats. As I went on to the pitch I was greeted with a mass of black and white going from the opposite halfway line, stretching around behind the goals at the Rangers end and running the length of the Main Stand.

ABER'S GONNAE GET YE!

There were also plenty of fans down from Tayside, but it seemed like Paisley had moved in its entirety to Mount Florida. The only covered area of terracing was housing Saints fans behind the goal and the noise emanating from it was already deafening. As I looked up to the Main Stand to find the full Clan Abercromby waving down at me, I though to myself: 'This is it! If you don't enjoy playing today, then chuck it. Look at those people – we just can't let them down!'

This was a view shared by all the players as we trooped back to the dressing rooms for the last quick team-talk. As this was going on, Frank McGarvey was geeing everyone up. He was the one player who had been there and got the T-Shirt during his Celtic career and a lot of the more impressionable lads were being inspired by his increasingly manic proclamations that: 'This is our day! United are bottlers! I'm telling you!'

As I followed Alex out of the tunnel to lead St Mirren onto the Hampden turf, my heart was bursting with pride. The roar of the crowd had got even louder and I felt remarkably at ease with the whole occasion. It was inspiring me - that is the only way I could describe it.

A new duty for me was to introduce the dignitaries to the rest of the players as we lined up on the touchline in front of the cameras. To demonstrate my lack of nerves, I decided to introduce my colleagues by their nicknames:

'This is 'Moon Man'.'

'Err…. good luck…. 'Moon Man'.'

And on it went until…

'This is Kojak'.'

'… Eh?... Good luck, Kojak.'

'Dibble'.

'Good luck. 'Dibble'.'

If you ever see footage of this incident, look at the reactions of my team-mates as we progressed down the line.

Pleasantries out of the way, it was now time for business. United was a very good team and en route to the UEFA Cup Final, had seen off top quality opposition across Europe, including a sensational victory over Barcelona in the Nou Camp. Understandably, they were favourites to beat us, but there were a few factors that people were not paying attention to. With a UEFA Cup Final looming four days after the Hampden match, there would be the temptation for the United players to not go into top gear, either by way of keeping some energy back for the Gothenburg game, or by trying to avoid injury and missing out on that occasion. After all, if they believed some sections of the media, they were only playing St Mirren.

Also, United had a horrendous record at Hampden with a grim catalogue of losing finals, sometimes when it seemed easier to win them. A living reminder of those nightmares would be on the pitch that day. Frank McGarvey's last contribution in a Celtic jersey before returning to Love Street was a injury-time winner against Dundee United in the Cup Final two years previously. Frank knew this would be preying on some minds and he was lapping it up!

I looked at their side as they warmed up. In particular, I examined the midfield: Bannon, McInally, Bowman, Sturrock. Every one an experienced pro and well respected in the game. I looked at our midfield of three teenagers - Fergie, Brian Hamilton and Paul Lambert - plus myself. If we weren't careful, we could be run over in midfield.

I quickly decided that one of the United midfield would have to be sent a message early in the game. McInally – he would do. A few minutes after kick-off the opportunity arose and I nailed him hard in a 50/50. To the untrained eye, it looked like no foul had been committed and indeed, ref Kenny Hope didn't blow. However, I knew that the bone-jarring collision in the tackle would have alerted McInally and his cohorts that I may be surrounded by kids, but Aber was very much alive and kicking. We were not going to be pushovers.

This may seem a wee bit unsavoury to some, but the simple facts are that in the hurly burly of professional football, this is how games can be won and lost. The United midfield never clicked into gear that afternoon and this was largely down to the way that the rest of the young lads followed my example and simply set about the opposition.

The overall game plan was to keep it tight and give the creative United players very little time on the ball to exert an influence. They had played a lot of games that season and we reckoned the longer the game went on the more tired they would become. We would then exploit that tiredness and the resultant gaps. Allied to that was United's infamous mental frailty regarding Hampden Finals and we estimated that they would start to panic the longer it went on without them being ahead.

ABER'S GONNAE GET YE!

At half-time it was locked at 0-0, with few chances to either side. Most observers thought that we would be quite happy at that point – they couldn't have been further wrong. Down in the St Mirren dressing room, trouble was brewing.

'Max - you're frozen man! Your like a f*****g rabbit in the headlights,' I bellowed at my young midfield colleague, Brian Hamilton. He sat and looked at me wide-eyed. I thought he was going to cry.

'Gaffer – take him off right now. His head is gone. I'm not going to let him ruin this for the rest of us,' I continued.

This was not how Alex had envisaged his half-time talk.

A voice piped up and it was Fergie's: 'You're right Aber.'

My reply was instant: 'You - you're just as bad. Yer heid's in the clouds son. Gaffer – take these clowns off now. Get Tony and Ian on. If you don't, then take me off – this is going to end in a shambles.'

Jimmy Bone's voice boomed out: 'Calm down Aber.' Then it was the turn of Alex Smith to demonstrate his quiet authority and infinite wisdom.

'Billy – enough. Everything will be OK. Give Brian and Ian another 15 minutes – they'll be fine. Trust me.' And then he got on with his critical team-talk. How right he was to be.

The second half went in much the same vein as the first and as time wore on, we grew and grew in confidence - especially my young midfield colleagues. Brian in particular was playing superbly and in the 90th minute, he almost won the tie when his right foot shot just flew past Billy Thomson's post.

As we jogged back I said to him: 'Could've won it there, Max. What was wrong with the left peg – would have been a cert.' Brian knew I was right, but also realised that I was not being critical and a knowing smile appeared. The boy was now supremely relaxed and he was soon set to make history.

Kenny Hope blew for the end of 90 minutes and extra-time beckoned. Jimmy Bone and Alex Smith came into their own here, with their two distinctly different personalities coming to the fore.

Jimmy went around firing up the players cajoling some, - especially Fergie, who was still misfiring - and using the arm round the shoulder technique on others such as Paul Lambert. Alex meanwhile was quietly going around the players giving each one of us specific instructions and encouragement. Then another voice chipped in. Frank – who else. 'Look at them. Look at the state of them.' And he was right.

While we were all still standing and buzzing with enthusiasm and an ever-growing belief that the trophy would be ours, most of the United players were slumped on the turf. Some were arguing amongst themselves, one player was physically sick and my old pal Jim McLean was wandering around them having animated arguments with his players. I knew then that we would win it.

The first half of extra-time saw nothing much change, but early in the second period, the match finally exploded. United broke down our right flank and a low cross was crucially tipped away from the feet of Kevin Gallagher by Dibble. The ball rolled to United's Iain Ferguson, who smashed it into the net and promptly set off to celebrate with the Dundonians on the terraces of the Celtic end.

My reaction was to look to the linesman to see if a flag was to be raised for offside, although in my heart I was sure it was a goal. The flag was raised – offside. Ya beauty! It really was meant to be.

Dibble's save was crucial because it prevented a certain goal from Kevin Gallagher, whose momentum then took him into an offside position on the goal line. Whether he was interfering with play or not is a moot point and nine times out of ten, the goal would probably be given. To add insult to injury, Gallagher was also flattened to the ground on the goal line by an onrushing Derek Hamilton.

I think that bizarrely, the whole incident promptly strengthened our belief and a couple of minutes later our date with destiny arrived.

I had the ball deep on our left and looked up to see a huge gap all the way down that side of the pitch. I hit a long ball up the channel, which Brian Hamilton deftly flicked through to Fergie, who had also seen the yawning chasm in United's defence.

For the first time in the game he was off and running. His first touch took him clear and as Billy Thomson came out to meet him, Fergie simply lashed a strike past his despairing dive and bulging the back of the net.

Hampden exploded and I swear the roof nearly came off the terracing behind the goal as thousands of Buddies went berserk. For everyone connected with St Mirren it was a truly magical moment – and still is.

Once the manic celebrations of the players had died down and some of us had run fully 60 yards to mob Fergie behind the goals – proof of the powers of adrenalin - the key was to focus on keeping our composure and seeing out the remaining ten minutes.

By now, Tony was on the pitch and he was inspirational to all of us, not just the young lads, in keeping things on an even keel. He almost scored as well, as did the other sub, Ian Cameron, who showed no ill effects from his morning university exams as he was denied only by a fingertip save from Billy Thomson from finishing off the game completely. United looked shot and there was very little reaction from them to the goal – if anything, we were getting stronger.

There was still a lot of tension and all I can remember from the final couple of minutes or so was Tony persistently badgering Kenny Hope along the lines of 'Hurry up and blow that whistle, Kenny… How long, Kenny?' and 'C'mon ref - that must be it'. Whatever Tony was doing, it seemed to work and when that nice Mr Hope eventually did blow his whistle, the joy was unrestrained.

It was heaven. The first person I saw was Tony. We had been on one Hell of a journey together for virtually all of our playing careers and we knew exactly what this meant to each other. The pain of all those semi-final defeats was instantly erased, in the full knowledge that we had achieved something historic.

Frank McGarvey soon joined us and the three old heads from the days of Fergie's Furies were finally united in triumph on the Hampden turf. Whatever our differences, we knew that something special had just been realised.

Conversely, I made a point of seeking out my old pal Billy Thomson – so deeply involved in the disastrous run of semi-final defeats and here he was being denied again - only this time by his old club and many former team-mates.

Football can be a cruel game and poor Billy could hardly speak to me such was his pain at the disappointment and the irony of the circumstances. I just gave him a hug and we went our separate ways. I couldn't say anything to make him feel better and I am sure that Billy also knew what the occasion was meaning to myself and his old colleagues from Love Street.

I just tried to soak it all in. The terraces were simply pulsating with noise and colour. I managed to get a quick victory wave up to Clan Abercromby in the Main Stand before the media surrounded me asking for interviews.

And yes, I was guilty of saying several times that I was 'over the moon.'

As I prepared to go up the steps to collect the famous old trophy, I savoured the moment. It was the realisation of a dream since childhood, of lifting the Scottish Cup at Hampden and as captain of the winning team, as well. I also briefly considered that seven months earlier, I had been banned for 12 games, stripped of the captaincy and transfer listed. Funny old game is football is another old cliché that is true.

The moment I lifted the trophy and saluted the tens of thousands of St Mirren fans was to be the finest of my career and I can only describe it as an unbelievable high.

It was back on to the pitch for more celebrations and a lap of honour with the trophy. Now the celebrations could really get going. Even the boys who didn't play that day, either through injury or non-selection, such as Big Basil, Gal and Paul Chalmers were running about overjoyed.

'Moon Man' had played with a pain-killing injection and as the champagne was being guzzled by all the players and staff, it was forgotten that his medication was not to be mixed with alcohol. Certainly not the best part of two bottles of champagne consumed in breakneck speed. Derek seemed OK, but as we all got out of the bath in the changing room, it was clear that all was not well.

He had to be helped out and poured into his suit, before being assisted on to the team coach. Blootered? Not even close. The 'Moon Man' was in his most spectacular orbit of all-time, on a heady concoction of adrenalin, a lot of booze and a sprinkling of prescribed medication. This was the beginning of a 48-hour 'trip' that would see Derek eventually sober up in Asia.

On the bus back to Paisley Town Hall, where thousands would fill the streets and the grounds of Paisley Abbey in a fantastic celebration - pubs were running at 1959 prices – the year Saints last won the Cup - I found myself at the front along with Alex, Jimmy, the Scottish Cup – and football commentator, Archie MacPherson.

The bold Archie was trying to record some interviews for that evening's highlights' programme, but unfortunately for him we had two other visitors on the bus - Frank McAvennie and Stevie Clarke.

The boys were delighted to be back from London in time to help celebrate the triumph and were at their mischievous best when I was trying to be the straight man during Archie's interview as we zoomed through South West Glasgow.

ABER'S GONNAE GET YE!

'Weetabix Heid – gie's a wave!' was one of the more broadcastable comments flying around the background as I tried to keep a straight face during Archie's interview. It was great to have the boys back – they were definitely part of the gang that evening.

Moon Man was by now becoming a liability. What do Kilwinning men do when in a moment of high spirits and triumphant partying? Why, they sing The Sash, of course. This was not going down well at the official St Mirren cup-winning function and Alex came over to me.

'Billy – you're his pal. You're the skipper. He's YOUR problem. Get rid of him - quick.' This will explain why some guests were astonished to see the St Mirren team captain, plus colleague Brian Gallagher carry an unconscious Derek Hamilton by his arms and legs, through the foyer and off to a hotel room where he would lie in oblivion until the next morning. It was still only 9pm.

The following day, we went on an open-top bus trip around a packed Love Street - where Derek Hamilton could be seen standing asleep on the top deck - before heading off to Glasgow Airport for a pre-arranged trip to Singapore.

The scenes in Paisley were astonishing with the ground being full despite the small detail that there was no game being played. Tears were shed, on and off the open top bus and the sheer joy in the faces of the St Mirren fans was something I will always remember.

This was a support that had only seen their team lift the Scottish Cup twice in their entire history and the sense of pride and joy was tangible. We felt like we were on some kind of crazy rollercoaster, as no sooner had we finished the lap of honour, than we were off on the short drive to the airport to begin the marathon journey to Asia.

We were playing in the inaugural EPSON Tournament, involving Southampton, Perth Azzuri, from Australia and Mexican team, Autonoma. We were all still buzzing from the Hampden success and flying to the other side of the world seemed to just extend the whole celebrations – we were now all going 'on holiday' together. It was to be one Hell of a trip.

At Heathrow, we met up with the Southampton squad and the two Saints set-off on a 14-hour drinking session at 30,000 feet. I think Derek was briefly in control of his faculties somewhere over Germany, but it was a fleeting moment.

ABER'S GONNAE GET YE!

On eventual arrival in Singapore, Southampton's ex-Liverpool midfielder, Jimmy Case, had gone missing. 'Where the bloody 'ell is Jimmy?' boomed Southampton boss Lawrie McMenemy, before bursting into laugher as he pointed over to the baggage carousel.

The air filled with a Liverpool accent shout of 'I'm a fooking CASE!' as Jimmy slowly made his appearance in international arrivals down the baggage chute, before going round the carousel on the conveyor belt waiting to be claimed. This was to set the tone for the trip.

We soon arrived at our Five-Star hotel, which was to be the base for the four teams. It had luxurious facilities and a nightclub within its walls. It was also the accommodation base for the contestants of Miss World, which was underway at the same time as the tournament.

So there you have it - four professional football teams away from home in an end of season tournament, locked up in a Five-Star hotel with the contestants of Miss World. Use your imagination – you won't even be close.

First up for St Mirren was a largely forgettable 0-0 against the Mexicans and all I can recall from that game was that we were really struggling in the severe humidity. The on-going post-Hampden celebrations probably didn't help either. The next day saw us draw 0-0 with Southampton, in a slightly higher tempo match, with my main memory being the previously mentioned competitive clashes with Jimmy Case.

In the third game, a 2-1 victory over Aussies Perth Azurri was achieved when a speculative shot from Kenny McDowall was spooned into the Perth Azurri net by their goalie.

Later that night, both teams were in the hotel's nightclub enjoying a few refreshments and the landscape provided by Miss World's finest. I saw that very same goalie on the dancefloor and in a fit of drink-fuelled bravado, decided to go up to him and start dancing in a manner that could only be described as p**s-taking.

As I mimicked his flailing at the ball, one of his team mates warned me to be careful saying the guy was 'a nutcase', but I didn't think there was a problem. However, there was a big problem on its way as I never saw the punch coming and was probably knocked out before my head hit the marble table beside the dance floor. Blood was apparently flowing freely from my head and an ambulance was called.

I came to in a pristine hospital ward, surrounded by Oriental nurses. Was this a dream? The unmistakable sounds of 'Moon Man' shattered my dream. 'Eh… Aber kid! Eh Doc… he's awake. Doc, Doc… is he going to be OK?'

I was indeed going to be OK. Just a few stitches in the gash in my head and a less than flattering shaving of the hairline as well. Once I realised that it was just Derek and myself, I knew the real pain was about to come.

'Has anyone told the gaffer?' I asked.

'Aye - the Doc's on the phone right now', replied Derek.

The doctor was phoning our hotel and was in the process of being patched through from reception to Mr.Smith's room - cheers Derek - at about 3am.

Doctor: 'Mr.Smith? This is the hospital. We have two of your players in here.'

Cue something like: 'Ye've f*****g whit?' at the other end.

'One of them came in unconscious in the ambulance from the hotel nightclub with a head injury and the other one was OK, but was there to accompany him. He is called Derek Hamilton and the injured man is….'

'Let me guess – Abercromby!'

'Yes sir, that's correct. Both men are ready to go home now. Would you like to come and collect them?'

Alex turned up a short while later, accompanied by Jimmy Bone. As I was wheeled out of the hospital by Derek - who seemed to be relishing his role as the innocent helper, but was fooling nobody - Smith and Bone gave me Hell.

To put it mildly, this was not the sort of example the team captain should be setting and what kind of ambassador was I proving to be? I had no quick comebacks – all I could do was prove my worth on the pitch less than 24 hours later. In the end, I was maintained as captain and went out to lead the team to victory in the final of the tournament. Again, we drew 0-0 with the Mexicans, but won 5-3 on penalties - I scored - to bring the trophy back to Paisley.

We had one other overseas trip to follow that summer. Benbecula may technically be overseas from Paisley, but only Ian Ferguson believed it to have exotic connotations. Alex knew the football people on the SFA's Highlands and Islands Committee and promised to take St Mirren over with the Scottish Cup. On the day of our departure, Jimmy Bone got a phone call from Ian Ferguson, explaining that he wouldn't be able to make the trip. 'I've lost my passport, Jimmy,' he said sheepishly. The nickname BOB - Brain of Britain - was well and truly cemented.

Domestically, my life was a bit of a car crash, but professionally, it could not have been better. After more than a decade of being a pro, I had achieved a lifetime ambition. I was also still team captain and there was the prospect of another European campaign - this time in the European Cup Winners Cup. This was the apex of my career. That summer, little was I to know how quickly it was all going to go wrong and send my life into a tailspin which would eventually almost result in my death.

11 The Road To Oblivion

"Drunkenness is temporary suicide."
Bertrand Russell

"I do not live in the world of sobriety."
Oliver Reed

"I'd hate to be a teetotaller. Imagine getting up in the morning and knowing that's as good as you're going to feel all day."
Dean Martin

FRESH from the successes of Hampden and Singapore, season 1987-88 began on a very optimistic note. Modest extra finance from the cup run had been spent on bringing in some pool players - and I don't mean Cool Hand Luke either - to augment the squad. Although there were still some injuries knocking around, we all shared the optimism of the fans that having finally won some serious silverware, the future was looking very rosy for St Mirren. As the team captain, I had extra reason to be enthusiastic.

As a warning of how things were about to stop going according to plan, just prior to the season, we were presented with our new playing kit. Clearly designed by Ray Charles and Stevie Wonder following a 20 pints of lager session, it was a hideous creation and the source of much black humour in the dressing room. The famous stripes were now pinstripes, with a huge big white panel on the chest to display the club badge and sponsor's name.

It was immediately christened 'the bib' – but in Gardner Speirs and Ian Cameron we already had some good dribblers at Love Street. Seriously, the design of kits doesn't really bother players, but this one was ground-breakingly awful. What actually bothered us was that it had a very tight collar

ABER'S GONNAE GET YE!

and appeared to have an insulated lining. Now this may help a fan on a freezing terrace, but for a player it was a bloody nightmare – especially in the warmer months - you couldn't breathe.

We started the season poorly and were knocked out of the League Cup, at home to St Johnstone. But we soon began to pick up our performances, just in time for another venture into European competition. Leading out St Mirren in Norway for our second-leg European Cup Winners Cup tie against Tromso, I was full of pride. We were back on the European stage again and hopefully this time we could progress quite far.

In the first leg at Love Street, a goal by Kenny McDowall was all that separated the teams, but crucially we hadn't conceded an away goal. The game was also marked by a bizarre incident where Jimmy Bone - allegedly - punched Frank McGarvey in the tunnel following Frank's substitution. Frank basically mouthed off at Jimmy as he was going off, 'Papa' followed him up the tunnel, a wee verbal spat ensued and Jimmy, who is not one to be messed with - again allegedly - put one on Frank. The following day, Frank threw his toys out of the pram and didn't play again for the first team for ages.

Jimmy wasn't - allegedly, for the third time - the first and he wouldn't be the last to stick one on Frank. Indeed, a couple of years earlier when Frank was at Celtic, I punched him to the ground whilst we were waiting for a corner. Frank had been p*****g me off all game and as we waited for Davie Provan to take the corner, something inside me snapped. Perhaps it had something to do with the fact we were being gubbed 7-1, but I punched the wee man. Down he went like a bag of spuds.

'What the f**k was that for Aber?' asked an incredulous Roy Aitken. The ref had missed it all – I wasn't that daft.

'Ach – he's been winding me up all game. I've had enough.'

'He winds us up too Aber, but we don't punch him.' laughed Roy, as Frank was led behind the goals by Celtic physio Brian Scott, blood and snotters covering the famous hooped shirt and the infamous, cherubic McGarvey coupon.

But back to our European adventures. Tromso were quite a useful outfit and I knew that we would have to be at our best to ensure a safe passage to the next round.

Less than half an hour into the game my season was over, my career was dealt a fatal blow and unwittingly, my life was about to be set on a downward spiral that would see me lose everything.

I had been having a problem with my Achilles' tendon and had only been able to play after being given cortisone injections – something that would never happen in today's game. All the drug did was mask the pain while the problem got even worse. I wasn't even training such was the pain, but I was needed by the team and was desperate to play.

During the warm-up to the game in Norway, I felt the Achilles beginning to flare-up again and was given another cortisone injection. In the middle of the first half, with nobody near me, I went down like I had been shot.

The pain was excruciating, but I tried to run it off. I got as far as five yards before collapsing again. My foot was just hanging off the end of my leg, lifeless. I later learnt that I had ruptured my Achilles' tendon. The tie had finished 0-0 and St.Mirren were through to the next round, but this was least of my concerns, although I was delighted for the management and the rest of the boys, as we were having a difficult start to the season.

And in a strange twist of fate, this was the same injury that finished Ian Scanlon's career when he came on as a sub in the tumultuous UEFA Cup win over Slavia Prague two years previously. Ian had come on as a sub, ruptured his Achilles' tendon 60 seconds later without actually kicking the ball and never played again.

I was scared, to put it mildly. A lengthy spell in plaster on the sidelines was the only guarantee at that point in time.

To make matters worse, this was my testimonial year at Love Street and the committee did a great job of organising a series of superb events for my benefit. The only problem was that I could take little part in things like golf days due to being in plaster up to my knee. At my dinner, Tommy Docherty was the guest speaker and he was fantastic. A real pro at that sort of thing, he had the audience in hysterics and at £600 for a half-hour speech he was very good value as well. Cheers Doc.

However, the sheer frustration at not being able to take part in the activities that had been laid on to mark my years at Love Street was not helping my mental state. Despite smiling on the outside, I was despondent on the inside as I hobbled around each of the events, every time accepting the platitudes and well-wishes of those in attendance.

Nobody meant anything other than well, but when the 500th person says 'What a shame - you in your testimonial year and all', I just wanted to scream: 'I F*****G KNOW!' But I didn't. I just smiled, thanked them and carried on hobbling around on crutches, my mind going round in circles as to the uncertainty of my situation.

Would I play again? Would I be the same player? Would I break down? Was it worth it? My mood was beginning to darken and fear was creeping in, creating the beginning of a paranoia.

With little to do but sit and wait in between physio appointments, I really did have too much time on my hands. Time to ponder my past, present and future. My family life was in tatters, largely of my own making and it was public knowledge. The career I had known ever since I left school/Great Yarmouth Butlins was now hanging by a thread.

From the unbelievable high of Hampden just 16 weeks earlier, everything I had known could be about to come crashing to a halt and I had little say in the matter. This feeling of hopelessness drove me to a very misguided form of therapy - the drink. Time on your hands? No need to be in tip-top condition? Feeling sorry for yourself? 'Go on, son - take a drink'. It was a route that was to have calamitous consequences.

On the pitch, the team was really struggling. Knocked out of Europe in the 2nd round – albeit to eventual winners KV Mechelen of Belgium, the league form began to go downhill as injuries began to pile up. To compound this, Ian Ferguson was sold to Rangers for a then inter-Scottish record of almost £1m. The sale didn't go down well with the St Mirren support, but Ian was getting a chance to play for his boyhood idols and quadruple his wages to boot.

Nobody at the club held it against him. In fact, his signing of a four-year contract at Love Street in the early part of the season almost certainly guaranteed St Mirren the massive pay day that the deal brought. I am certain that both St Mirren and Fergie knew a deal was in the offing and to get him to sign that contract was a smart piece of business by the Love Street board and a decent thing for Ian to do.

Unfortunately, the Saints fans always held the episode against him and it is sad that the scorer of the cup final winner remained for so long a bad guy in the eyes of the fans. I know that Ian loved his time at Love Street and thought highly of the club and his colleagues.

With Fergie gone, plus Tony suffering a knee injury and myself also injured, the midfield was very exposed and this wasn't helping matters. As defending winners, we were knocked out of the Scottish Cup at the first time of asking by Clydebank. Relegation was a very real possibility. I tried to make a comeback, to try to help the team out. In my first reserve match, the tendon went a second time. I would never play for St Mirren again.

As the club began to spin into a depression, although that didn't come close to the way I felt, the Board pressed the panic button. Less than 12 months after winning the Scottish Cup, Alex Smith and Jimmy Bone were sacked. This was a massive shock to all the playing staff, especially the younger lads who really looked up to Alex and Jimmy.

A few tears were shed when they came in to break the news and say their goodbyes and even I felt a lump in the throat. What was to follow was even more surprising - Tony Fitzpatrick was appointed manager, with Frank McGarvey the assistant manager. Neither had any coaching experience at senior level, but were tasked with keeping St Mirren up. Talk about a gamble. It worked though and a 1-0 win at Tynecastle, ending Hearts' 12-month unbeaten home run - oh how they must have loved St Mirren - saw Tony and Frank achieve their initial task.

The appointments of two of the three old heads as the new management team and my exclusion left me feeling angry and confused. I wasn't angry about not being asked to be manager or assistant, but I was team captain and had passed my coaching badges at the celebrated SFA courses at Largs.

I wasn't even asked about joining the coaching set-up at Love Street and it hurt. I was crocked and I got the feeling that senior management at Love Street thought my career was over – despite the fact that medical advice wasn't quite as damning as that. My overall mood blackened and I entered a spiral of self-destructive behaviour that would run for years.

I was now living in Kilbarchan with a girl called Elaine Henderson or 'Gadget' as I affectionately called her. Ironically, just a few doors away from Peter Donald who was a known face to me as he was regularly on the SFA's disciplinary panels.

Faced with another long spell in plaster and totally demotivated by the recent events at Love Street, Elaine had to play the role of friend - and psychiatric nurse. Thanks Elaine - my Lady In Red - I owe you for all your help, as I must have been a nightmare to live with. I couldn't walk. I couldn't train. I was basically housebound – just a cross ball from The Trust Inn, the village's pub.

Looking back, this was the period where I began to make the jump up from full-time social drinker and weekend alcoholic to full-time alcoholic and not a very sociable drinker. I had tons of time on my hands and nothing to do. I was depressed. I drank. A lot. I was more than happy to sit and talk to folk of all walks of life and always had done during my career.

Being a well-known local footballer didn't make me some form of higher human life form. I was just an ordinary guy and I loved to share the patter with the man on the street. It's a wee bit different these days, but I think that is a shame, as players become even more distanced from the fans who pay their wages. However, this period was different. I was getting hammered on a daily basis and the wheels were definitely coming off the Abercromby lorry.

I now ask myself almost every day - how did I become an alcoholic? Where did it start? I cannot pinpoint it exactly, but the Kilbarchan era is definitely when the problem/illness began to take serious root.

I had always been a play hard, party hard guy. As a professional footballer, there was ample scope to burn the candle at both ends and get away with it, provided you were prepared to put in the physical toil at training, something I was never scared of.

Also the regime of game after game, followed by a wee break in the summer, followed by a gruesome pre-season schedule – it all acted as some kind of regulatory process, where alcoholic intake was cleansed out by physical rigour and further controlled by the fact that you simply couldn't drink around game times. We were a successful team and we had a lot of fixtures – this also helped keep me in check.

Laid-up in a living room of a small village, immobile and cut off from most of my team-mates, who had become second family, I chose this as the time to accelerate the drinking as there were no training sessions or matches to worry about. My mood was black, not black and white.

Alcohol seemed like the best medicine to cure me of my collection of ills - the physical pain from my injuries, the chronic boredom - I knew nothing other than playing football, or training to play football, the erosion of my self-confidence and the depression that was overtaking me.

I don't mean depression in the sense of 'Jings, I feel a tad glum here'. I mean depression when you believe everything is going wrong, you don't have a future, life is over as you know it and that I might as well cash in my chips – that kind of depression filled every waking hour.

Every day I woke up was like Groundhog Day. Go to training? Nope. Go for a walk? Nope. See anybody? Visit the family? Nope. Get good news about a comeback? Nope. Career over? Probably. Ten Pints of Guinness before tea-time? Sounds just grand to me. So off I would hobble to The Trust. Until they banned me – for longer than the SFA did as well and it hurt almost as much. This was getting out of control.

On one occasion, I freaked out in my house and chucked my crutches through the front window. CRASH! Straight through the glass, sending debris onto the pavement outside.

A couple of minutes later there was a knock on the door. It was an old lady who had been passing by with her shopping from the local grocer's. 'Have you lost these son?' she enquired. I politely thanked her, took the crutches and shuffled back through to the sofa. This was madness – I had to get fit. I had to play again.

As I approached only my second reserve match in a year, I was informed that Partick Thistle wanted to sign me as a player-coach. I was very, very interested. Jags' manager John Lambie saw enough in that reserve match to make a firm bid for my services, but there were a few complications. I was still due my Testimonial match, which was to be against Newcastle United, at Love Street. Also, I was still under contract at St Mirren, on a deal that Thistle couldn't quite match.

I felt that I was owed something by St Mirren for more than 12 years service and was not prepared to leave until a settlement could be agreed. It felt odd talking about this in a cold business-like fashion with my old pal Tony, but these were the harsh facts of life as a professional footballer.

Eventually, a settlement was agreed, probably hastened my agreeing to waive the Testimonial match – something I have regretted, as it would have been a great occasion and a perfect way to say "farewell" to the fans.

To demonstrate how much faith he had in me and almost in complete reverse to the views held at Love Street about my fitness and career longevity, John Lambie signed me for Partick Thistle in November 1988, on a two-and-a-half year deal, as player-coach. Although it meant dropping down a division, the move took me back to within kicking distance of my old Possil stamping ground and in a strange way it felt like I was coming home despite my inward devastation at having to leave Love Street.

There was a great bunch of characters at Thistle. Guys like Gordon Rae – a man-mountain experienced centre-half, striker Gerry McCoy, full-back Alan Dinnie, former Saints colleagues Brian 'The Madman' Gallagher and

Gary Peebles. And last, but certainly not least - James Callaghan 'Chic' Charnley.

Chic was one of the most skilful players I have ever seen and we had already played together as he had started his career at Love Street before being shown the exit door. I'm not sure why he was transferred as his abilities were superb – as good a left foot as you'll ever likely see. Unfortunately, Chic was 100 per cent mental - probably why Saints sold him - and there was never a dull moment. The only guy who seemed capable of handling him was Lambie, who had brought him to Thistle after the pair worked together successfully at Hamilton Accies.

Unfortunately, my Thistle career got off to a very bad start and this was to be a sign of things to come. My debut was at Firhill against Kilmarnock. Dropping down a division, I was a big name with a big reputation according to Lambie and I was warned to expect to be targeted for some treatment from opposing sides.

This didn't worry me in the slightest as I had more than held my own against some of the toughest guys in Scottish and European football. In the dressing room before the Killie game, the lads warned me that Killie's midfield hard man, Gordon Wylde would almost certainly be out to get me. Bring it on was my reply. It certainly was brought on. After only 28 minutes, a loose ball fell between Gordon and myself and we both went for it – the difference being that the ball was of secondary importance to either of us. We both knew that we were going to try and do each other. I got there first and collided with Gordon's knee on his standing leg. I am not sure if I got the ball. Gordon was pole-axed and in agony. I was quickly surrounded by Killie players literally after my blood. The ref immediately sent me off.

Lambie was furious and made clear to me his disgust. We were not off to the best of starts. A couple of weeks later, I phone Gordon at his home to apologise. His wife answered: 'Gordon - it's that bastard Abercromby.'

Gordon came on the line and was OK about it, admitting that he was trying to do the same to me. I guess I was too experienced at that sort of thing – dealing with the likes of Souness and Kenny Black was a Hell of an education. Unfortunately, Gordon was part-time and lost his job as a result of the injury. Even worse – his career was over.

I had a huge amount of sympathy with Gordon. We both knew that it could have been the other way round and I began to ponder how everything I had ever known could just be cut short in a second. A moment of madness or bad timing – either way, it could easily finish your career. However, if you start to dwell upon this for too long, then you will simply be unable to play the game properly, always thinking 'what if', playing at greatly reduced commitment levels. Your career would be over pretty damn fast that way as well. I did feel guilty – it was only natural, but Gordon's honest appraisal of what happened did ease this.

I was given a three-game ban and as soon as it was up, I was stripped and ready for a second appearance for Thistle. At about 2.30pm, Lambie came in the dressing room:

'Take your playing gear off Billy – you're not playing.'

'What?'

'No chance Aber. You're not playing today.'

Lambie than thrust the team sheet in front of me. The referee? Louis Thow – my personal nightmare from the three red cards against Motherwell. It was clear that John thought that my disciplinary problems were a liability and that having Thow as ref would be the footballing equivalent of walking on thin ice. Nonetheless, it was a defining moment for me at Thistle. If this was his regard for one of his coaching staff, then I knew my days were already numbered, before I had even got started.

One bright spot in my Thistle career came a month or so later when we were drawn against St Mirren in the Scottish Cup 3rd round. I didn't play in the first game, a scrappy 0-0 at Firhill, which Saints should have won when my old pal Peter Weir - who had returned to Love Street, from Leicester City - was blinded by the low winter sun as he attempted to guide a cross ball into an unguarded net. I was delighted - no offence, Peter - as it handed me a chance to have one final run-out at Love Street.

A few days later, a very large and noisy crowd piled into Love Street for the replay. I was a sub and it was customary for the away team subs to do their warm-ups during the match at the Caledonia Street end of the ground, in front of the visiting fans. I was having none of this and went around to the Love Street end to do my warm-ups.

The reaction was absolutely fantastic and the match action seemed of little interest to the fans. 'Aber's Gonnae Get Ye! Aber's Gonnae Get Ye!' sang the Buddies and as it got louder and louder, reverberating around the ground, I am not ashamed to say I was a wee bit emotional. Even the Jags fans were joining in. Eventually Lambie pitched me into action for my last ever game on the Love Street turf. We ran out 3-1 winners, knocking Premier League opposition out of the Cup, so I have no apologies for looking so pleased at full-time. However, the reception I got that night will live with me forever.

Unfortunately, this was to be the only real high point of my Jags career, as another bizarre episode was about to put an end to any working relationship I had with Lambie and the directors.

The deal I was on at Thistle wasn't quite what I was earning at Love Street. Although I was player-coach, training only took place on Monday, Tuesday, and Thursday evenings, which left plenty of time free during the week. I got another day job with the full approval of Partick Thistle as a sales manager for car showroom giants, Arnold Clark. I was in charge of vehicle parts sales for Ayrshire and it was a good job, getting around the country, meeting some nice folk and making a few quid while you were at it – so far, so good.

The problem was, I had forgotten to get signed off as claiming Invalidity Benefit from the DSS. I had been receiving payments to supplement my income during my 12 months out injured at Love Street, as appearance bonuses etc. were unavailable due to my long-term injury.

As soon as I was fit again and with the new contract at Thistle, I should have signed off. When the payments kept coming, I just thought, 'Why not?' and believed that the authorities would never come calling. Even if they did, surely it would be no matter for the courts, as I wasn't getting much in top-up benefits anyway. This was a bad error of judgement and in retrospect, sheer stupidity on my part.

In the end, someone – probably a disgruntled Thistle fan – shopped me to the authorities and I was quickly up in court to be found guilty of falsely claiming invalidity benefits whilst employed as a professional footballer. Another first for Aber in the annals of Scottish footballing history. The episode was well chronicled in the closing pages of Stuart Cosgrove's excellent book about the underbelly of Scottish football - Hampden Babylon - where the tale was accompanied by photos of Dalglish, Souness and Stein – at least I was in good company. As Stuart put it: 'Show the Scots a social security form and we'll show the world a fiddle.'

This was the final straw for Lambie and at the end of the season, a mere six months after joining, I was put on the transfer list. To say it wasn't working out is a bit of understatement. But what happened next was a surprise to everyone – least of all myself.

Newly promoted to the top flight, Dunfermline Athletic were looking to build a strong squad of players. Former colleague, Ian Munro was the No.2 to Pars boss Jim Leishman. Ian got in touch having heard about the demise of the Jags Experience and I was offered a full-time contract on some of the best wages I had ever been paid. It also meant I would be back in the top-flight, having been written off by so many. So, I was off to Fife like a shot.

It was an excellent squad that was being assembled: Goalie, Ian Westwater; 'Mr.Dunfermline', Norrie McCathie as a towering centre-half. Norrie was to tragically die a few years later while still playing for his beloved Pars, following a gas leak at his house. There was John Watson; ex-Rangers and Northern Ireland star Jimmy Nicholl and young Irish striker George O'Boyle who was all set to make a name for himself in the Premier League.

Last, but certainly not least was Doug Rougvie. Finally, I got to play in the same team as Doug – a relief, as it was always more preferable than trying to deal with his competitive style as an opponent. Doug would play just behind me, so if anybody managed to get past Aber, then they had Doug waiting to deal with them. Thou shalt not pass.

We started the league well and went top after a few games. Around this time we embarked on a League Cup run that took Dunfermline to a Hampden semi-final against Rangers. Unfortunately, a Trevor Steven-inspired Rangers team demolished us 5-0.

A few weeks later, just prior to a clash with Rangers at Ibrox, I found myself in a spot of bother with the law that almost resulted in me being unable to play due to being in the holding cells, at Paisley Sheriff Court. It wasn't the first time and it makes grim reading.

12 I Fought The Law And The Law Won

DRINK-DRIVING CHARGE NO. 1

It was on 4th December 1983 – the birth of my daughter Candice. I was scheduled to play for Saints away at Kilmarnock, but this was obviously dependent on when Anne-Marie went into labour. I cracked a few jokes about inducing her so I could make the game, but unsurprisingly my audience at the hospital was less than welcoming to the idea. Eventually, nature ran its course and I phoned the manager, Ricky McFarlane to let him know that I couldn't make the trip. Ironically, my beautiful wee daughter was born at 3.05pm on the Saturday – to have gambled on playing would have been one of the worst decisions of my life.

On the Monday at training, I was snowed under with presents from all the players and staff at Love Street. I decided to put them in the boot of my car, before heading off to the Southern General Hospital to see Anne-Marie and Candice. Lex Richardson and Frank McDougall were with me and said hello to Mum and baby before going back to the car to wait for me.

We then set off for a snooker club in Glasgow that Frank was a member of -'Luther' was a big fan of the game and a good player as well. At the club, we had a few refreshments, before heading off to drop the presents off at my house in advance of a wee celebratory bevvy session to wet the baby's head. En route to my house, I went through a red light – right in front of Partick Thistle's ground - and a Police car.

As the inevitable failed breath test took place, Frank and Lex started taking the policeman to task in the middle of the street, asking that he cut me a bit of slack given the circumstances. It was futile and wasn't really helping, as the shouting got louder and more aggressive. As I was bundled into the back of the police car, my team-mates simply gave me a big thumbs up and shouted: 'We'll look after the pressies', pointing in the direction of my now abandoned car. As I was driven off in the police car, I looked round to see them wandering into the nearest bar, laughing their heads off.

Result: £100 fine and a six-month ban.

DRINK-DRIVING CHARGE NO. 2

Late 1987 and just out of plaster. After another furious row with Anne-Marie at the house in Lochwinnoch, I drove off on the Renfrewshire back roads to my house in Kilbarchan. On the way, I flew past a parked police car. I'd had a couple and knew that it could be ropey if I was caught. To my dismay, in the rear-view mirror, I saw the police coming after me, blue lights illuminating the unlit country roads. Despite the fact it was snowing, I floored it and quickly lost them – or so I thought. My next fatal error was to drive to my house, park the car outside and jump in the passenger seat, pretending to be asleep. When the Police duly arrived to throw the book at me, I was fooling nobody.

Result: £200 fine and a 12-month ban.

DRINK-DRIVING CHARGE NO.3

Just prior to Christmas 1989. On a Thursday afternoon, after training at Dunfermline, I was driving home to Kilbarchan. We had the Friday off, as we were due to play Rangers at Ibrox on the Saturday. I was still in my Dunfermline tracksuit when I made the error of deciding to go via the Fox and Hounds pub in Houston. I only had two pints, but that was enough to put me over the limit. The area was notorious for people drink-driving back from the local pubs and at that time of year police checks were common. At 5pm I was pulled over and inevitably failed the test – again. I knew that this time I really was in the s**t.

After being charged, I was sent to the cells at Paisley's Mill Street Police HQ, to await my hearing on the Friday. My fellow cellmates were so out of their faces on drugs that nobody worked out who I was – the Dunfermline tracksuit may have confused their fragile state of mind. After a sleepless night, I was standing in the dock.

Arsenal defender Tony Adams had just been all over the papers after being jailed for drink-driving and this was my third charge. I was feeling less than optimistic about making the following day's game – Dunfermline were blissfully unaware of the whole episode – and anticipated a wee trip to the Bar-L (Barlinnie Prison, in Glasgow). This time I copped an 18 month ban plus a £300 fine, with a warning that if there was any further repeats, then I would be guaranteed a custodial sentence.

Phew - I'm a free man - or so I thought, but it wasn't that simple. I didn't have any cash or a chequebook on me and couldn't pay the fine. I was still to be locked up, this time in the holding cells at the Sheriff Court. Frantically, a number of phone calls were made -I thought you were only allowed one - to get my lawyer to withdraw £300 from my bank account before the banks shut at 4pm and then get down to the Sheriff Court to pay the fine. Any delay and I was to be kept in the cells for the whole weekend. Ibrox would be an impossibility and an immediate sacking from Dunfermline a very strong possibility.

Fortunately, my lawyer came good and I was able to take my place at Ibrox. I did tell Leish about being caught, but decided to miss out the bit about being jailed and coming within five minutes of being banged up while I was meant to be taking Gary Stevens out the game in front of the Govan Stand. Only now am I coming clean about the whole sorry saga and I send my apologies to all involved at East End Park during that time.

A short while afterwards, I started to have severe pains in my pelvic area and it ended up where I was in agony from even walking, let alone playing football. Medical advice pointed to wear and tear from years of playing and I was given two options - an operation to solve the problem – but with no guarantees of success, or to stop playing for a period of six months to two years to allow for a natural recovery of the problem area.

At the age of 32, time was not on my side and I opted for the operation. By the time I was nearing the end of my period on the sidelines, it was clear that Dunfermline no longer wanted me. They clearly felt that I was a crock and I was surplus to requirements. Being a professional footballer is a fantastic way of life, but sometimes it can be so very, very cruel. With little explanation, I was shown the door at East End Park. This was also soon after I had sold my house in Kilbarchan and bought a house in Fife, so the timing was pretty bad. This house in Fife was to be my base for the next five years - a period that would see my personal and professional life collapse like a the proverbial pack of cards.

Fortunately, I had a few ex-colleagues who were starting out in

ABER'S GONNAE GET YE!

management, who offered me part-time contracts – the only problem being that I really needed a full-time deal. Jimmy Nicholl took me to Raith Rovers for three months. Following that, I spent short-term contracts at Cowdenbeath, then East Stirlingshire. Things were getting grim. Jimmy Bone was now manager of Airdrie and gave me a short-term deal at Broomfield, which gave me one final chance for a crack at the big boys. We were playing Rangers and in their surprise at seeing me line-up for Airdrie, Ally McCoist and Mo Johnston wandered over in the warm-up.

'Hey Aber - any chance of going easy on Mo and me today?' asked Ally in his usual cheeky fashion.

'Away and chase yersel'.'

'Tell you what Aber - don't boot us up in the air and the drinks are on us tonight in Vicky's.' (an infamous Glasgow nightclub)

Some night we had in Vicky's I'll tell you.

At the end of the Airdrie deal, I was still desperate for a full-time contract. My knight in shining armour was the unlikely figure of Jim Leishman, recently sacked at Dunfermline. Leish was installed as manager of ambitious Highland League team Inverness Caledonian. One Friday afternoon I got a phone call to the house from Jim. Fortunately he wasn't talking in riddles for a change.

'Are you fit, Billy?' he asked.

'Aye.'

'So how's about it then?'

'It'll cost you. I need a full-time deal.'

'No problems and you can holiday wherever you want – as long as it is in Inverness.' That was Jim's way of saying that digs would be laid on as well.

Inverness was more of a social outing rather than a football experience for me. Jim had assembled a gang of nutters, ably led by himself and he seemed to be enjoying every minute of it. On one occasion, we were away at Peterhead and it was seriously sub-zero weather. As he finished his team talk with another joke - and by this stage, the jokes and anecdotes were getting more airtime than the tactics - he looked out of the window at the appalling conditions, looked at us lot wanting to be anywhere but there and started singing Always Look on the Bright Side of Life. Encouraging us to join in, he proudly led his boys down the tunnel, with the entire squad singing the Monty Python classic. We won, after scoring three goals in the first 15 minutes. There must have been some method in Leish's madness after all.

After my year in the Highland League, the summer of 1993 saw me sign for Junior side Rosyth. A full seventeen years had passed since I turned down Fergie's offer of playing in the Juniors, but I was still proven correct to turn him down. Whilst Rosyth were an ambitious wee club and had just opened a new stand, the action on the park was the footballing equivalent of Mad Max – Beyond the Thunderdome.

Each side was awash with nutcases that would have made Gregor Stevens think twice about playing. And to make matters worse, being an ex-pro, I was a marked man. A full 20 seconds into my second game, I had my collarbone broken by a tackle so late, nobody in the ground even saw it. However, after getting fit and playing again, I finished the season with Rosyth, amazingly with all limbs still intact.

Around this period, I began teaching physical education at Hillside School, in Fife. It was a residential school for problem kids from all over the East of Scotland. These were the kids that nobody wanted - expelled by schools; discarded by families – the kids simply had nothing to lose and didn't care about anything. Authority meant nothing and it was a seriously scary place. I came up against some fearsome opponents on the pitch, but none of those guys came close to the boys and girls of Hillside House.

I had kids threaten me with screwdrivers, jump over the desk for a square go and generally try and intimidate me in ways that nobody had ever tried before - not even Graeme Souness. I remember with great pride that I was able to handle these situations and calm the kids down, even getting them to eventually join in and make valuable contributions to the activities we were organising.

Even if it was just basic PE, they seemed to get a lot out of it and as a consequence, so did I. Back in the school days in Possil, I had hoped to be a PE teacher if I never made it as a player, so here I was living the dream, albeit not in exactly the circumstances I would have planned for.

At this time, I was involved with a smashing girl called Yvonne Holmes. Yvonne was a gem and someone of whom I am still very fond of to this day. She had a wee boy called Mark and I helped raise him as if he was one of my own. The sense of having a second chance at having a proper family life was a welcome respite from the downward spiral of my playing career, but it only proved to be a temporary pit-stop on the road to Hell.

Eventually, Yvonne could take no more of my boozing and the negative impact it was having on her and Mark. I was given an ultimatum - change my lifestyle, or lose her and Mark. The fact that such a challenge was put forward only serves to highlight the ludicrous nature of my behaviour. My answer simply confirmed it - I chose to leave.

I knew I couldn't change – the lifestyle, the drinking, the mentally abusive behaviour I was subjecting them to. Any fool would have chosen the alternative. Yvonne was a wonderful girl and Mark was every inch the adorable wee boy. However, the logic of every fool pales into insignificance when compared to the thought processes of someone who has been well and truly grasped by alcoholism.

Denial? No chance – I wasn't in denial. I was embracing it. I loved the drink and it was now completely taking over. To Hell with the consequences and whoever I may hurt. To Hell with the rest of my life. I wanted no commitment to anything other than the bottle. To an alcoholic, just like a heroin addict, nothing else matters. You only have one sincere and genuine relationship that matters, but just like everything else in your life, you ultimately p**s that away as well. Finishing with Yvonne felt like someone was cutting free the only remaining lines between me and the real world. The um-Billy-cal cord had just been cut.

I still had some hunger for the game, but to be honest, I was just working for the cash to fund my alcohol addiction. I had no inclination towards crime and my only foray into fraud had already seen me arrested and charged. In the summer of 1994, I signed for Kilbirnie – another junior team. A few games in and a fan was picked to make up the numbers in our starting eleven - and he was the best player. I quit football the very next day. This was the bottom of the ladder and I knew it.

To top it all off, I had to sell the house in Fife to pay off a massive overdraft and was now back in Milton – back where it all began almost 20 years previously. The journey started on Balmore Road, took a turn to Paisley and its pleasant leafy satellite villages, followed by a sharp detour to Fife before landing back at square one.

I had the princely sum of £50 in my bank account. Not a massive amount for almost 20 years as a professional footballer, playing in Scotland's top league, representing my country, playing against the cream of Europe and being only the third person in history to lift the Scottish Cup for St Mirren.

Fifty quid, no family, a trail of broken friendships and no career to speak of for life after the playing days. I simply couldn't handle it and felt like I had nothing to go on for. Life as I knew it had come to an end. I might as well hit the bottle and go out in a blaze of glory. The thing is, there is no blaze of glory, just a horrifying mess. I had been all over the world as a player, but now I was set to go on a journey to some Hellish existence and what's more, I wanted to.

Pondering my next move, I was made aware that as I was now 35, I would be able to access my SPFA Pension fund. The arrangement was that when you got to 35, you could:

a) Start getting monthly payments from the fund;

b) Take a slight lump payment and get reduced monthly payments;

c) Get the whole fund paid out as one lump sum, with no further monthly payments.

I took option c), collected my £50,000, set the controls for oblivion and pressed the ignition button on a 13-year-long binge where I would lose everything, before almost killing myself. My drink problem was already bad at this point. My decision to sign a one year contract with a 12 year option with serious alcohol abuse was simply the inevitable next step.

I'm not going to preach at anyone. I'm not going to say 'don't drink'. This is what happened to me. It was all my own fault, but it could happen to anyone else. It could even happen to you.

Initially, it was like one long party. The pubs and clubs of Glasgow and Paisley were my playground and I went for it 24/7. With the big bucks of my pension burning a hole in my bank account, it was party time and I was footing the bill for anyone who wanted to join in.

Of course, this attracted hangers-on, who were more than willing to capitalise on my largesse, but I didn't care. It just meant that there were plenty to party with and hang on my every word as tales of the good old days rolled out in each and every bar and nightclub we visited.

Paisley was always a great place for me to visit, with no shortage of people wanting to have a drink with me and revel in the not too distant memories of the glory days. By this time, St Mirren were virtually bankrupt and sliding to the bottom of Division 1 - a long way from the heady days of 1977-87.

My life was empty, but Paisley was a place where I would be welcomed by old friends who remembered who I was and what I had achieved with St Mirren.

These alcohol-fuelled days and nights in Paisley kept me in some form of protective cocoon from reality. When a pub full of people are chanting your name – despite the fact that you can hardly talk through intoxication – and are happy to keep buying you more and more drink, then you can see how the place quickly became like a Wonderland for me.

The sad irony was that in the midst of all this hero worship and celebration, I was publicly beginning to shatter many people's impressions of me. It's hard to still be an idol, when you are incoherent at 1.30pm on a Monday afternoon. Christ knows what some of the fans must have thought of me back then, but at the time I didn't give a s**t.

Soon I was garnering a reputation for letting people down at St Mirren. Kenny McDowall had a testimonial game and part of the evening was to involve a game between fans who had paid to play and a Saints Old Boys XI. Starsky, Luther, Doug, Becky, Lex – they were all there, showing that they had not lost any of their touches. It was great to see them, but some of the boys seemed concerned at my physical and mental condition. I was meant to play in the game. I arrived late and several sheets to the wind. I cracked the old story about Alex Miller and the collapsing wall and this cut the tension, but I knew that I had let the boys, the fans and Kojak down. This hurt like Hell, but the feeling only wanted me to obliterate it with more drink, so off I wandered back into Paisley. I never even saw the end of Kenny's big night.

A couple of years later, St Mirren supporters organised a charity game to raise much needed funds for the ailing club. It was the tenth anniversary of the 1987 triumph and people paid for the chance to play on the Love Street turf, this time against the 1987 line-up. I agreed to play - but that is about as far as I got.

I travelled to Paisley, met up with 'Moon Man' Derek Hamilton with the intention for both of us to get down to Love Street to help out the good cause and meet up with some old friends. When the game kicked off, the 1987 captain and his full-back colleague could be found in the Station Bar, completely off our faces. When our actions sank in, I felt the sense of shame and immediately went for the bottle to wipe it out. For me drink was the answer to all of life's ills – but the cause of them as well.

My next steps towards the lower levels of Hell was when the money began to run out. It had only taken me three years or so to drink my entire pension fund. The pub and club circuit would need to come to an end. This didn't really bother me – there were cheaper pubs nearer to home and failing that, there were my old pals whom I used to see down on the canalside. Nightclub or park bench? I didn't care – I just needed the fix and the surroundings were irrelevant.

The first sign that the endless treadmill of pubs and clubs was hurtling out of control was probably when my place of residence for a while was in a barn near Inchinnan. This was no farmhouse redevelopment into luxurious accommodation. Nope. It was a working farm which belonged to a farmer known as 'Old MacDonald' and I was living in a wee room built on to the side of the barn. 'Old MacDonald' had a pet ram that used to use his horns to bash me awake from my drunken slumbers each morning. What I was doing there I can barely recall. All I know is that by this stage, I was operating on a different planet from the rest of the normal human race.

Soon after, I moved into a rented, one bedroom flat, back in my native Lambhill. It was in a state of disrepair and a far cry from the leafy, country retreats of Lochwinnoch and Kilbarchan, but it was all I could manage. At least I was back home. Better still, I was living above an Off Licence and I set into a routine that was to be the benchmark of my existence:

Morning:

Wake up. Splash some water on my face. Have a drink of water and a cup of coffee. Perhaps nibble on whatever foodstuffs were lying around the flat. Go downstairs to the shop for breakfast - a bottle of QC Sherry. I would then take some bread down to the bird sanctuary on the canalside tow path out of Glasgow towards the Campsie Hills and feed the birds. Then I would meet up with the other wildlife on the canal side, 'The Crazy Gang' and we would have our public meeting for the remainder of the morning. I was Chairman.

Lunchtime:

Back to the shop for lunch - a bottle of QC Sherry. Then back to the public meeting – see who is still alive.

Teatime:

Walk back to the flat, stopping off at the shop for evening meal - a bottle of QC Sherry.

I did this for more than ten years. Think of that next time you see the Christmas adverts for QC Sherry, with groups of socially adjusted people swapping nibbles and chat beside an open fire at some party. I guess my lifestyle wasn't quite what the advertising executives had in mind for the brand, but trust me, QC is one of the most popular weapons of choice for the serious alcoholic. Quite Charming the adverts would say. Quietly Choking is more apt.

Ironically, the lady - called Shurinda - who owned the off-sales where I bought my QC Sherry has become a very good friend and has supported me in my battle against the booze. This is despite a sharp drop in her profits thanks to my abstinence.

Prior to being taken to hospital, I was prone to having seizures and they had been happening with increasing regularity. In fact, the local paramedics were getting so annoyed at having to walk all the way down the canal side, before pushing me all the way back to the ambulance, that they actually said: 'Can you not go bevvying nearer the road?'

It is a piece of black humour that actually masks what really happened when the drink got its final grip on me. This is what some experts refer to as the end game for alcoholics - a frantic paranoia that forces the addict to consume more and more until the brain and/or body physically collapse under the strain.

In the second half of my decade of QC insanity, I was suffering badly, both mentally and physically. The seizures were being brought on by alcohol withdrawal. Any prolonged period of not drinking – and by that I mean less than 24 hours – would see me collapsing to the floor without warning, shaking violently and literally foaming at the mouth, whilst my eyes would roll up into my head. Not exactly a pleasant sight.

The seizures frightened the Hell out of me. There was no warning and I knew virtually nothing about them, other than when I came round in hospital, it was a case of thinking 'not again' followed by a relief that I was still alive, although I do use that word loosely to describe how I was at this time in my life.

I was drinking every waking hour and an advanced state of intoxication became my default mode of appearance and behaviour. Where it starts to get really heavy is that to the outside world, I often seemed fine, perfectly coherent and in control of my faculties. I wasn't – I was literally out of my mind, but this had become so much of the norm that I began to be able to function quite well, to the extent that some people were unsure whether I was on the booze or not.

This is simply another stage of alcoholic madness taking over – being drunk is the normal way for you to be. Not being under the influence is when you start to freak out. This is why you often hear of people who were able to hold down jobs for years on end, despite the fact that it eventually comes to light that they were consuming a bottle of Vodka every day, during working hours. It was the Vodka which was keeping them 'normal' in everyone else's eyes.

I was once in the Argyll Bar, in Paisley, which was a usual haunt for me when I fancied an exotic trip away from the Lambhill Canal Crew. My pal, Gerry went up to the bar. 'What do you want Abs?' he asked, his voice trailing off when he turned round, shock taking over as he witnessed me lying on the floor in the middle of the pub having a seizure.

I remembered walking into the pub, the next thing I recall is waking up in the hospital 24 hours later. This was becoming the normality of my life. I once managed to have three seizures in one day, only being taken to hospital after the last one, with the medics being certain that I wouldn't see the night out.

This soon gave rise to alcoholic madness - if the seizures were being brought on by alcohol withdrawal, then I needed to avoid withdrawal, otherwise I would have another seizure and I might die. It was the alcoholic's guide to survival.

The lunacy of this logic still makes me chuckle darkly today. The fear got to me – I needed to ensure I was on the bevvy all the time. And I mean all the time - from the moment I woke, to when I collapsed some time later. I was now in the firm grip of a vicious circle, which is the usual final killer of alcoholics.

I drank so heavily that any attempt to avoid alcohol brought on seizures. To avoid the seizures, I drank even more. There is simply no other outcome from this circle, other than the inevitable demise. That can often come without any warning as well. One of the canal boys went home for his lunch and never reappeared. When the police broke his door down, he was found in a pool of blood on his floor. His liver and kidneys had virtually exploded and he had died a quick, but excruciating death, probably choking on his own blood, but hopefully he had a heart attack before it got too bad. That is the effect that alcohol abuse has on you.

ABER'S GONNAE GET YE!

Next time you read about some celeb going into a Five-Star retreat for rehab, don't be kidded. They are probably miles away from the real, horrible, addiction that has no future other than a certain death and a miserable, painful one at that.

Those that are shuffling around the Priory in their embroidered dressing gowns are probably still well within the reaches of being saved - unless they don't want to be.

People become addicted to drink or drugs for many reasons. For some, it is a deep-rooted desire to opt out from normal life and escape into a wee world of their own. They don't want to be saved. They don't want to come back. Unless you really want to come off the drink, then you won't. Chances are, you will die.

I didn't want to come off the booze - I was trying to kill myself and I knew it. It was my family who forced the issue by effectively kidnapping me and dumping me in hospital.

13 Walk The Line

AUGUST 2007. I am in a ward with three others in Stobhill Hospital. They all died while I was there. The place was basically a hospice for alcoholics. Looking at my fellow inmates was all that kept me going. I'm not going to die… I'm not going to die was the mantra going through my head. My intestinal system was shot to Hell from the years of boozing and I couldn't eat – I was kept going on a combination of protein shakes and intravenous drips. I had severe jaundice and was also covered in rashes as my body seemed to be going into some kind of shock.

I was frantically scratching like a flea-ridden hound, drawing blood, or what was left of it, from sores opening up across my body. Pain? Nothing. My body was completely numb as if my senses had shut down. I couldn't sleep and being cooped up in a room with three poor souls wasn't helping – the conversation wasn't much either.

One day the doctor put a camera down my mouth to have a look around the toxic wasteland of my insides. I was shown a picture of my liver – it was completely black, bar a tiny little piece of pink in the corner.

'See this little pink quadrant? This is what is keeping you alive,' he tells me. 'Any more drinking and I mean any more drinking and this will fail. You will probably die a very painful death. If you do manage to avoid alcohol, then this pink quadrant will regenerate and the longer you stay sober, the more it will regrow and the healthier you will become. At the moment, there is absolutely no margin for error. Your next binge WILL kill you. Do I make myself clear?'

F*****g crystal.

Other than the doc's blazingly obvious logic, something deep inside me clicked into gear like some kind of emergency self-preservation device. I wanted to get off the drink. This was my last chance and I knew it. I wanted to survive and I knew that this desire would be critical to the success.

At nights I used to walk backwards and forwards across the few yards of the ward. I would do this for hours on end, like a dog locked up in a kennel. I thought my head was going to explode. One night a nurse came over:

'Mr Abercromby - could you please stop that. You'll wake the others up.'

'They're already dead,' was my cutting response, before I begged her for a sleeping tablet. Eventually she relented, but this was the only night I would sleep.

My parents came to see me in hospital – just in time to witness another seizure. I can only imagine what was going through their minds at the sight of me writhing there, in a ward that should have been called The Waiting for Death Ward. I was their first born son and it shouldn't have been like this for them. Afterwards, I made my mind up – I was getting out of here and fast. My first 'escape' was definitely not with medical blessing.

Mary, the landlady of my local pub The Inn heard a loud knock on the door just after closing one night.

'Who's there?'

'Aber.'

'Whaaaat?'

She opened the door to find me in NHS pyjamas, paper slippers and a dressing gown and caked in mud. On closer inspection, I still had the IV entry tubes attached to my arms. I had broken out of Stobhill Hospital and had walked the three miles home as the alcoholic crow flies. This took me straight across a golf course and it would appear that I had more trouble than a 36 handicapper navigating the fairways. I was the walking and living embodiment of someone both desperate and dying for a drink.

I asked for a dark rum which was duly poured and the police were called as well. All I did was sit and hold the drink, my hands shaking. I stared and stared at the dark brown liquid for ages, but not a drop passed my lips. I was too scared to go any further. Strathclyde's finest soon arrived to provide my taxi back to the Ward. The next escape plan would need to be smarter.

My sister, Elaine was getting married the following week and I wanted to be there, whatever the implications to myself.

When I told the doctors of my plans, they said I would be mad to do this, with the general inference being that if I left the hospital, then I would soon be back - in the mortuary. But I wasn't having any of this and sensing that I was still hovering close to life's exit door, I didn't want to miss the wedding.

I walked out of Stobhill Hospital, two weeks into a six-week recovery programme. If I was going straight and giving up the drink, I was going to do it my way. Doing cold turkey in Possil is about as far away from celebrity rehab as it is possible to get – but probably twice as effective and several thousands of pounds cheaper.

I made the wedding and kept a low profile. My new short haircut and removal of the vagrant chic beard, probably caused me to slip past most people unnoticed, but I was equally aware of many pairs of eyes drilling into me and people whispering behind my back. To be fair, I wasn't exactly looking well and some people either thought I was dead already and they were looking at a ghost, or thought I was just about to snuff it. As soon as the music started at the reception I was off. It was too much for me and I headed straight for a place that I knew would be empty on such a family occasions – my parents' house. Anyway, I had my own life-changing journey to embark on.

Cold turkey was both physically and mentally harder than anything I had ever endured during all my years as a player. Chronic insomnia was accompanied by constant sweats as my body felt like it was burning up on the inside. Rashes appeared all over my body and I was shaking so much you'd have been forgiven for thinking I had Parkinson's Disease.

I would lie in bed, wide awake, my mind racing. I was soaked in sweat, with a screaming in my brain - the panic attacks were beginning to appear. It felt like the walls were closing in on me and I was suffocating. I jumped out of bed to punch and kick the peeling wallpaper and exposed brickwork, the walls of the dirty old flat threatened to close in and crush me. A while later, everything would calm down – for a while, at least until the next night. This was a living Hell – was I better off on the bottle?

I can now see why so many people fail in their attempts to come off booze. Anyone who thinks that it is just down to beating a craving is deluding themselves. A serious alcohol problem is akin to coming off heroin. The withdrawal process doesn't just test your physical resolve, but worse than that is the mental torture. You just don't see any way out.

Improvement doesn't seem noticeable and this gives way to depression and anxiety attacks, for which the default reaction was to take a drink – and I don't mean Lucozade.

The only thing that kept me going was fear. The knowledge that one more binge would kill me constantly nagged at the back of my head. I was becoming more aware of the real world again and felt that I had unfinished business.

Never mind myself, I owed it to those friends and family who had stood by me, I owed it to those I had let down so badly – I had to give this a real go. I am utterly convinced that the years of gruelling pre-seasons and constant hard training had given me the physical strength to still be alive at this stage. Anyone with a more mundane, less athletic background would have been in a box long before now. Perhaps I could use my career one last time – this time to save my life. Now I had to apply the mental strength that had become my forte when taking on the toughest of the football world.

Ultimately, the success of anyone recovering from severe alcoholism is down to the individual themselves. Help from friends and family is great, but effectively worthless unless the patient wants to recover. The physical and mental agonies of the recovery process cannot be borne by well wishers. They can keep your spirits up (bad pun, I know), but only you can have the required desire and strength of mind, body and character to pull through.

George Best simply didn't want to stop drinking. The alternative was too frightening for him. The recovery too much of a horrible process, so he drank until he died, despite the love of his family and the best medical support that money could buy.

As I write this, Paul Gascoigne looks to be heading the same way. He has rejected all help from friends and family and is on a single-minded mission to blot out the rest of the world and to Hell with the consequences. Sounds familiar? Unless Paul really wants to get clean himself and I suspect he doesn't, then I don't see any happy ending. I sincerely hope I am wrong.

Deciding to make a genuine attempt to get straight, I adopted the mentality of approaching the equivalent of my toughest ever pre-season training programme. I couldn't eat, as my digestive system was in a bad way, so I had to manage my own programme of prescribed medication and supplements.

Honestly, I probably rattled every time I walked down the street. Food supplements, vitamin shots, diabetes medication, liver function tablets, sleeping/coma tablets – all were coursing through my veins at the same time, where weeks earlier my blood stream was 100% QC.

I went to one AA meeting at a local church. I found it incredibly depressing and it further strengthened my view that only an Abercromby Regime of cold turkey was the way I would beat my demons.

Initially, I stayed at my parents' house for two months. Looking back, this was terribly unfair on them as my medical problems and almost manic sleeplessness were far from over. The trouble was my flat nearby was just too close to canal side and all my old buddies. I was scared to come home – it was too dodgy. Being the loving parents that they are, my folks looked after me and helped get me on an even keel so I could face the outside world.

I was petrified and I am not ashamed to admit that. I knew the journey ahead would be hard - a life without booze, a life that initially was empty without the bottle, as prior to me being in hospital booze was all that mattered to me. Family, friends had all come a distant second and I was worried that I may not be given any opportunities to show people that I was trying to get straight.

The one thing that hits you when you are recovering from alcoholism is the sheer amount of spare time that you have – it is this that can often quickly lead people back on to the drink. I was determined to use the time to try and re-establish contact with the outside world and rebuild my life as quickly as possible.

The brain was working again and I was encouraged to keep a diary. It was a simple idea, but very effective. In the beginning, the pages were blank, but quicker and quicker I wasn't just recalling my feelings, but actually using the diary to book in appointments and meetings – simple proof that I was turning my life around and getting reacquainted with what is recognised as normal society.

My old pal Gerry Docherty, a talented footballer, who had a successful career in England and Australia, was also an equally talented artist and had done a marvellous painting of St Mirren playing Celtic at a packed Love Street. Gerry thought it was my 50th birthday and wanted to give me this surprise gift. It sure was a surprise, not least because it was actually my 49th birthday, but I'll let Gerry off as I looked about 80.

Anyway, once we had had a good laugh about it, I decided to auction it for Radio Clyde's Cash for Kids charity appeal. As bad as things were for me, I wasn't feeling sorry for myself and thought it might be a good idea to get some points in the karma bank in advance of my struggles ahead. In the end, the painting went for several hundred pounds to The Bank pub, in Paisley and I was there with Gerry and Tony Fitzpatrick to hand over the artwork to the generous landlords.

It may come as a surprise for some, but I have always been very active in charity work, but I never liked to talk about it. In the 1980s, I was approached by a Paisley man, Peter Rafferty, who is President of the Affiliation of Celtic Supporters Clubs. In between organising the masses of green and white, Peter's life was touched by tragedy when his eight-year-old son, Paul died from a rare brain disease. It was a human tragedy that puts all of life's troubles into the correct perspective.

Peter set about a massive fundraising campaign for special brain scan equipment at Yorkhill Sick Children's Hospital, in Glasgow and approached me to get involved. I was a well-known face in the Paisley area as one of Saints' higher profile players and also had links to that part of Glasgow as well. I was delighted and honoured to help and Peter went on to become a big part of my life and an inspiration to many.

The actual charity work was great fun. Five-a-side competitions, beat the goalie, darts tournaments, golf days, raffles in pubs – anything was undertaken to get the funds rolling in and I had a great time helping raise money. A huge amount of money was raised and the contribution from the people of Paisley could never be underestimated, especially as the town's population had an undeserved reputation for being able to peel an orange and not take their hands out their pockets.

What was even more fun for me was that as I was the representative of St Mirren, I was coming into contact with many other representatives of the Old Firm, whom Peter had also coerced into getting involved.

Paul McStay, Brian McClair, Willie McStay, Mo Johnston, Ally McCoist and Davie Provan were just some of the guys I would meet up with at the fundraisers and their reaction at meeting me off the pitch was always quite amusing.

For most, their only meetings with me was picking themselves off the ground after a trademark Aber tackle. I think I was viewed as some kind of psychopath, which probably explains my reputation within the game and they were all quietly taken aback when meeting me for the first time in a non-football capacity. Here was Aber – the person and I think my general laid-back, cheery disposition came as a surprise to these guys. They used to look at me as if something was wrong. Was I feeling alright? Why wasn't I growling at them? Where was the foreboding menacing presence? The myth was shattered and we all got on really well - until the next time our paths crossed on the turf.

I've been only too happy to help out others less fortunate than myself. It is hugely rewarding and something that I continue to do to this day. A year after he did the first painting, Gerry managed to do another superb one for my 50th birthday. This time it was of the Saints against Dundee United to commemorate the 1987 Cup Final. We managed to auction it for hundreds of pounds for a Breast Cancer Charity, in Paisley. In a moment of madness, I promised to wear a pink suit to a fundraising event, but fortunately the organiser, Evelyn Campbell never held me to it. I'll leave that kind of sartorial elegance to Macca.

Auctioning the painting kind of put me back on the map in terms of public awareness of my existence. The Chinese whispers had basically had me as dead and that wasn't too wide of the mark. The response from everyone to the news that I was back in the land of the living was astonishing and a real welcome surprise for me.

Over the previous decade I had let so many people down that I was almost afraid to make contact with faces from the past. Worse still, I couldn't even remember the exact details of what I had done wrong, but I just knew that I had let the side down - big style. Would anyone want to deal with me again?

First step was to renew contact with my two beautiful daughters, Candice and Hayley. I had been a terrible father up to that point. Virtually non-existent and when I was around, there was a fair-to-middling chance that I was on the bevvy. More than anything, this is my deepest regret about that whole period in my life and the pain that I feel about it still hurts. You cannot re-wind the clock, so all I could hope for was to try and finally be a proper Dad to my girls.

While their mum, Anne-Marie and I no longer get on, which is quite understandable on her part, I have to pay credit to her for raising two wonderful, beautiful children. They are bright, funny, caring and have a terrific love of life. Candice is a qualified music and drama teacher, as well as an opera singer and Hayley is a forensic biologist.

I am immensely proud of them both. The fact that the girls were prepared to give me another chance is largely down to the values that they were raised with and for that I am extremely grateful. One of the major landmarks on my comeback was receiving a Father's Day card from them with some genuinely touching words written inside the card. I'll treasure that card to the day I die.

The next step was getting back into my old flat and getting it into a condition for human habitation. Previously, it was virtually a hole where I would sleep off binges, before heading out again. With the help of some close friends, the place was transformed into a nice, smart modern abode - something that would have been well beyond the means of Changing Rooms that's for sure. Instead of Carol Smillie and co. the work was organised by my two pals Yvonne Farlow and Carol Mungay. These two have done so much to help get me back on track that I simply don't know how I can ever repay them.

They even organised to take me for a wee holiday to Spain. This was another huge step in my rehabilitation, being in the sunshine for seven days surrounded by people drinking alcohol. It probably isn't the sort of recommended treatment I would have got from the NHS, but as Yvonne, Carol and co. set about testing every cocktail known to man, I managed to keep on the Coca-Cola.

As the sun shone down on that wee spot in Murcia, I knew that I was well on the route to recovery. Your friends can help you on the road to recovery from alcoholism, but ultimately the success stands or falls with the individual. You have to want to succeed. It becomes an obsession and I began to enjoy setting the tests of strength to my character and ignoring the risks that would lie ahead should I fail.

Next up would be interesting - St Mirren. Other than my family, this was the biggest part of my life. Since finishing playing, I had become a well-known face in the bars of Paisley, talking football with the fans. I loved those sessions, but as my drinking got worse and worse, so did my behaviour and I was now of the opinion that many supporters would have thought of me as an embarrassment and that the club would want nothing to do with me.

St Mirren had tried to induct me into their Hall of Fame at an annual dinner, but I was uncontactable - I think you know what that really means and Tony Fitzpatrick went up to get my award 'posthumously'. When St Mirren won the First Division in 2000, a mass celebration was held outside

Paisley Town Hall. In the mass of fans below, the last man to captain them to a Scottish Cup Final win could be found toasting Saints success with a bottle of sherry and a straggly beard. I recall nothing of this, but this was not how I wanted to be remembered by the Saints support.

A couple of pals, 'Big Fras' Kirkwood and even bigger Bill 'Pavarotti' Ross started the process of re-acquainting me with St Mirren - the club and the fans. I was genuinely astonished to find that the Club Shop was selling 'Abercromby – St Mirren Legend' T-Shirts and that a supporters' website was also selling 'Aber's Gonnae Get Ye!' T-Shirts. Maybe I wasn't the forgotten man after all.

Alan Provan, who was running the club shop, kindly gave me a copy of the 1987 Cup Final DVD. It was a very strange feeling watching it, as all the memories began to come back. A feeling of tremendous pride was tinged with sadness as most of my old colleagues were interviewed in the current day reflecting upon the triumph.

Where was I? Again uncontactable. Oh dear. My contribution was my on-pitch interview with BBC Reporter Reevel Alderson, which was littered with classics such as 'I'm over the moon' and the chillingly bad prophecy that 'great things were around the corner for St Mirren'. It was great for my parents and daughters to see the DVD and I was delighted to be able to show the girls just what their old man used to do so well.

Most bizarrely, I was made aware of a song in my honour, written by Paisley musician Al Mitchell. The Ballad of Billy Abercromby was a great wee track and as I write, is still available for your delectation on Al's website. The lyrics sum up my career at Love Street perfectly and I eventually got the chance to thank Al in person when we met up in the players' tunnel at Love Street. I wish him every success in his musical career – a truly talented individual and a good guy as well.

ABER'S GONNAE GET YE!

THE BALLAD OF BILLY ABERCROMBY (© Al Mitchell)

Billy came through the ranks at St Mirren
Signed full-time in '75
Sir Alex Ferguson gave him his debut
He was a man ahead of his time

Chorus
Ooh Billy.... Ooh Billy
This is the Ballad of Billy Abercromby
Ooh Billy....Aber's Gonnae Get Ye!
This is the Ballad of Billy Abercromby

Billy gave 13 years to St Mirren
He would fight for every ball and he would win
The opposition wouldn't mess with Billy
If they did….he'd be in!

Chorus

On the 29th of October 1986
Motherwell came to Love Street
Billy got into a fix

Oh Billy….Oh Billy
The ref he sent you off 3 times
Oh Billy…. Don't do it Billy
We didn't think we'd see you again

Billy came back and captained us to glory
It was May 1987
We won the Scottish Cup
And Paisley was in heaven

Ooh Billy…. Ooh Billy
This is the Ballad of Billy Abercromby
Ooh Billy….Aber's Gonnae Get Ye!
That was the Ballad of Billy Abercromby

ABER'S GONNAE GET YE!

We made contact with St Mirren and Commercial Manager, Campbell Kennedy kindly organised for me to be a guest at their next home game against Falkirk. The reception I got within the various hospitality lounges was amazing, bettered only by being taken on to the pitch at half-time to get the cheers of the fans as I was finally given my Hall of Fame award. It was an emotional moment. I must have made a good impression, as St Mirren were gubbed 5-0 and I was awarded Man of the Match and given, would you believe, an engraved glass tankard. The irony wasn't lost on me and both awards are safely on the mantelpiece of my flat.

Other than my scrapbook, lovingly created over the years, these awards are about all I have to show for my career. All the medals and memorabilia disappeared during the lowest levels of my alcoholism. People ask me about the 1987 Cup Final medal and shirt and therein lies a couple of tales. When I was living in Kilbarchan, I decided to put the medal in a safe place and planked it in a cavity between the fireplace and the wall. When I left that house, I was so out of it that I forgot to take the medal. While we were writing this book, I took a trip down to Kilbarchan to try to find the medal. The owner of the house had some bad news – the medal was nowhere to be found. There had been a bad flood in the area a few years back, and the house had suffered quite a bit of damage. All the floorboards had to be replaced, and there was quite a bit of structural work carried out. I can only assume that the medal fell down the back of the fireplace and into the foundations when the work was going on. You never know they might put a wee blue plaque outside the house saying 'Billy Abercromby's 1987 Scottish Cup Winners Medal lies here… possibly'.

As for the shirt I wore on May 16th 1987 – well this is one of the few things I am bitter about. I was a regular in The Tile Bar, in Paisley and one of the regulars was always nagging me about seeing my Cup Final top. One day I brought it in. 'Here you are, ya old bugger,' I said throwing the jersey at him. 'Get us a pint of Guinness and you can keep it.'

It was meant as a joke, but I was also in steep alcoholic decline, something that must have been noticed by the man in question and the staff of the pub. When I next came back to the pub the regular had never brought the top back and the next thing I knew was that it was hanging on the wall of the 19th Hole bar in Renfrew.

Most of what happened to me was my own damn fault and I am not chasing sympathy from anyone, but this was different. Hopefully one day

ABER'S GONNAE GET YE!

I can somehow get the top back, as it is something that I would love to hand down to my daughters and for them to pass through future generations.

I got back in touch with some old pals from my playing days and their genuine delight in seeing me back on my feet was a real tonic - without the gin, naturally. I often see Tony and 'Starsky' at St Mirren games as well as many others from my playing days, either at the game in a scouting capacity, or simply along to enjoy the match. There are some high quality line-ups in the stands these days – its just a shame about the fitness levels.

On one occasion I bumped into Frank McGarvey in the main stand at Love Street. He was curiously attired, with a big fedora-style hat and outsized sheepskin jacket drowning his wee frame. I had a chuckle as I remarked to myself that he looked like a cross between Malcolm Allison and Deputy Dawg.

Anyway, as I approached him, I casually said: 'Alright, Frank?'

'Aye,' he casually replied, before turning away. The wee sod didn't recognise me.

'Nice hat, Frank. I hope it fits.'

'What? Is that you, Aber?' Then the penny finally dropped. We blethered away for a while, before heading for our respective seats. Two minutes later we were reunited again – Frank had tickets beside me. He was there scouting for one of Saints' upcoming opponents and as per usual supplying a constant commentary on the game and the shortcomings of the players, throughout the first 45 minutes.

Some things never change in life and Frank's rock solid self-confidence was still resolute after all these years. In the second half, the McGarvey commentary continued unabated, but it became clear that he had a wee problem. He had forgotten his glasses and was struggling to make out the numbers and names on the back of the shirts as he tried to compile his report. I saw my chance to have one final piece of fun at Frank's expense and best of all, he wouldn't be able to get a word in.

'Who's the big number nine, Aber?'

'Eh, Jim Hamilton.' It was, in fact, Billy Mehmet

'Who's that number ten? Is that Dargo?'

'Aye.' It was Dennis Wyness. Craig Dargo was still sitting on the bench about 20 yards in front of us.

And so it went on until Frank went away with a marvellous piece of fiction representing his scouting report, containing at least three players who weren't even on the pitch. Sorry Frank, but it was too hard to resist.

One thing that I took delight in was being presented by The Scottish Sun newspaper to young Stephen McGinn, who in October 2008 became the first St Mirren player to score a winning goal against Rangers for 22 years. Guess who scored the winner back then? Yours truly. I told you I only scored important goals.

It was great to be sharing the celebrations with another generation of players, although it did make me feel old. Stephen wasn't even born when I scored the winner in 1986. This was just 12 months after I came out of hospital and to see myself across the back pages of the papers was a final confirmation of my progress.

Correction. The final confirmation came from my doctor, following a full check up of my condition. An annual MOT for the body was the best way of looking at it. I passed with flying colours.

'Billy, you probably have a better liver than I do,' he said. It was music to my ears, but more than that, it felt like the greatest victory of my life. You cannot kid these people – any form of alcoholic intake would have shown up straight away, but I had followed the orders, disciplined myself and created my own programme of getting back into shape.

It is still hard and to use an old cliché, it really is a day-to-day process. As the days turn into weeks and the weeks into months, I am not ashamed to admit that for the first time in years I am proud of myself. I can see it in the eyes of my loved ones. My beautiful kids and my dear parents – they are so pleased with the way that I have turned everything around from the brink of death. It is their reaction and being able to share their lives that drives me on every day.

I still go down to the canal, but only to feed the birds, or go for a bike ride as I try to build up my fitness. Occasionally, I'll stop and talk to the canal side crew, or at least what is left of them, as six have died since I went straight - the youngest aged just 32 - all from alcohol-related complications.

But it is a glimpse into a previous life and is enough to remind me of what could have been. I don't ever want to go back there, back to that Hellish existence. The overall feeling is that I have lost ten years of my life, but I am back and raring to go again and there is so much left to do. We are only passing through and I have wasted enough time.

The anger I feel at this passes when I think of the future that lies ahead

– life is full of opportunities if you look hard enough and I am revelling in the sense of freedom that I now have.

I still have my coaching badges and believe that I could offer something back to the game, maybe within the senior game, or maybe helping others who have fallen off the line with their lives and are using sport to help get themselves back together.

Who knows what the future holds, but one thing is for sure, I am winning my battle and am determined to make up for lost time. Be it friend or foe, one thing is guaranteed – Aber's gonnae get ye!

Epilogue
The Beginning Of The End.... Or The End Of The Beginning

DURING my years in the alcoholic wilderness, it wasn't just me who was going downhill. St Mirren had ended up being relegated and in a financial mess. It finally ended up with only one way out to safeguard the future of the club - Love Street would be sold to Tesco and a new 8000-seater ground would be erected half-a-mile away in Ferguslie Park. It was a situation that nobody wanted, but a necessary evil to keep the club afloat and give them the possibility of a bright future. After going through what I have endured, I could relate to the situation.

The memories of Love Street would always remain - the Fergie revolution, winning the Anglo-Scottish Cup, Cruyff, Gullit, Dalglish, Best and Co. playing at Love Street, the great goals and wonderful victories, the heartbreak of Hammarby and the night it all went wrong with Louis Thow.

The superb support I received from the Paisley faithful for over a decade meant so much to me that when I visited the ground and closed my eyes, I could still hear the chant ringing in my ears – 'Aber's Gonnae Get Ye! Aber's Gonnae Get Ye!'. I still get a lump in my throat even thinking about it.

I can only imagine what the old place meant to the fans, especially the loyal hardcore, who have followed the team through the good years and the largely garbage years that followed. They may not be the biggest support

ABER'S GONNAE GET YE!

for any team in the world, but you simply cannot buy passion like that and in many ways Saints are a superbly supported team. I just wish more people would come along and watch them, but if a successful team is put together, then the Paisley public will get behind them – eventually. It just might need Fergie to get in his Bentley with his loudhailer and drive around the town again.

However, all good things must come to an end. The new ground at Greenhill Road coincides with Saints' best run in the top flight since I hung up my boots. Current manager, Gus MacPherson seems like a good guy, always accommodating to me when I pop round to the ground and is also learning the ways of the Paisley public's occasionally unrealistic demands for success.

Football has changed a lot since the glory years of 1977-87 and finance plays a massive part in how far up the league teams finish. The new ground and improved facilities will hopefully help Gus and the team rise and repeat the successes of my time at the club – nobody would be more delighted than me to see that. I may have been a Glasgow boy, who idolised the Lisbon Lions as a child, but St Mirren is my team – make no mistake and as a fan, I only want the best for them.

In recent times, Campbell Kennedy has been kind enough to provide me with tickets for games and I still feel the buzz when I am coming into the ground on match days. There are always well-wishers and one bit I always enjoy is bumping into groundsman, Tommy Docherty.

He's always busy, but never fails to take a moment to stop and have a wee chat with me. Tommy was a smashing guy, the kind of unsung hero who is worth his weight in gold to any club and he is part of the very fabric of St Mirren FC. I don't want to get him in any trouble, but Tommy used to get 'Moon Man', myself and many others out of scrapes with club officials and I'll never forget it.

Chairman Stewart Gilmour and Vice-Chairman, George Campbell are always giving me a warm welcome and it is probably rare in this day and age where the guys running a top flight club are just as big fans as the rest of the punters coming through the turnstiles. On more than one occasion I've been told by the directors to get out on the pitch and play - all a bit of fun, but it means a lot that my years of service are still recognised. I wish I could take them up on the offer, but in these days of TV evidence, I probably wouldn't get far.

Anyway, as the days disappeared to the final match at Love Street on January 3rd 2009 - against Motherwell, my old friends from the Thow incident - there was a growing media interest in the whole affair and I began to find myself in demand. This was so heartening, as I was basically a lost cause only a year earlier. A documentary was made about Love Street and I found myself being interviewed for that, along with doing some Press to support its launch. I was just grateful that people had remembered who I was and that I was still alive to be part of it. To be recognised as a St Mirren legend was so uplifting for my own morale and self-esteem, that I thought I should be thanking those guys and not the other way round.

Next up was Chick Young – a real gent and a true Saints fan, despite how he is portrayed in other sections of the media. I met Chick in the tunnel at Love Street just before the team ran out for a game against Celtic. Chick was doing some media work and was asking if I could be interviewed for a Radio Scotland documentary on Love Street. Naturally, I was delighted and we fixed a date.

Just then, a familiar figure emerged from the Away Dressing Room – my old nemesis Gordon Strachan. During our playing careers we had a love/hate relationship – I loved to hate him and the feeling may have been mutual. As Chick switched back to his day job covering the game, he shouted: 'See you later Aber.'

Strachan, who had nodded at me seconds previously, not recognising me, did a double-take. Our eyes met and everything just stood still for a second. A cagey: 'Alright?' was exchanged, but there were no smiles nor greetings of long-lost colleagues. It was like we were back on the pitch again at Love Street, Pittodrie, or even the Scottish Cup semi, at Parkhead where I was sent off for sending Gordon on to the running track. The same place where he would, in the future, be seen bouncing about like a madman in a Celtic tracksuit as manager - an image that seemed impossible to comprehend in the 1980s when he was just about number one hate target for the Celtic support. Some would say that view still remains among a section of the Hoops' fans.

When the radio show was broadcast, Chick did a great piece about me as a character and I appreciated his words. The show ended with yours truly saying how much the fans seemed to appreciate me and that I appreciated them in equal measure. Enough said.

In the weeks leading up to the final game, the club announced that former players wishing to attend should contact Stewart Gilmour and that some form of reunion was being organised. This was too good an opportunity for me to turn down, as a chance to finally meet up with all my old colleagues and let them see for themselves that I was very much on the comeback. It was to be an emotional day for all concerned, in many different ways. Not just the former players, all meeting to swap stories and memories, but for the 10,000 fans who packed in the ground one final time and let their minds wander off to all the moments they had shared and experienced over the years in that wee corner of Paisley.

I was excited to be meeting up with the guys again, with the added intrigue that I had no idea who would all be there – maybe there would be some faces to avoid. How would everyone be faring? Who was or wasn't feeling the strains of time and were some people still crazy after all these years.

On the day of the game, I pulled in nice and early to the car park, just in time for Stewart Gilmour to offer me his car parking space and warmly shake my hand. On this day of all match days, it was a nice gesture and helped confirm what a good guy he really was.

There were loads of people already arriving, despite it being two hours before kick-off and the odd cry of 'Aber's Gonnae Get Ye' was sent in my direction, accompanied by huge smiles and thumbs up gestures.

I was buzzing and the adrenalin was kicking in – this was the closest I had felt to actually playing in a long time. My pal Gerry Docherty - who is Lex Richardson's brother-in-law and had been an active member of the Saints infamous social scene of the 1980s was with me and we were directed round to the Caledonia Street end.

There now stood a modern 3,000 seater stand, complete with hospitality bars, gymnasiums and five-a-side pitches. Back in my day, it was just a sweeping bowl of uncovered terracing, usually lying empty until the Old Firm rolled into town.

We used to train on the vast expanse of grass that lay behind the goal and the perimeter wall, but now the stand was right up at pitchside and seemed to heighten the atmosphere at games when it housed a large away support.

We were amongst the first guests to arrive at the reception for former players. It was no surprise that someone had already beaten us to it – Derek Hamilton. The 'Moon Man' had come out of hiding in Stewarton for the occasion and with the promise of a chance to meet up with old pals, wild horses couldn't have held him back. The free bar may have helped motivate him as well.

I ordered my usual soda water and scanned the arriving guests, searching for old colleagues. Soon they began to arrive in droves. Ian Cameron strolled over and warmly greeted me. He was now working as an accountant in Glasgow, proof that taking his exams on Cup Final day wasn't so mad after all. Nothing had changed with Ian – literally. He still looked about 21. His son was with him – I thought it was his brother.

We were quickly interrupted by a bear-like hug from a red-faced, barrel-chested man with white hair - and it wasn't Santa Claus making a detour on his way back from handing out the Christmas pressies. Dressed like a French Resistance fighter clad in black overcoat, scarf and flat cap – Jimmy 'Papa' Bone. The first time we had met for over 20 years and the sense of humour was still firing on all cylinders. He greeted me like a long-lost friend and the feeling was mutual.

I looked around the room and saw Gordon McQueen talking in one corner; Stuart McCormack, the old club Doctor who used to fill me full of cortisone was talking in another and the air was crackling with laughter and bonhomie. My old pals were everywhere: 'Starsky', Lex, John Young, Alan Logan and Frank McGarvey - we were all soon chatting away reminiscing about our exploits, taking in Paisley and stopping off in Finland, Brazil, Sweden, Holland, Czechoslovakia and Singapore.

I turned round and bumped into Tommy Wilson, now on the staff at Rangers. He brought best wishes from Kojak and Ally McCoist who were otherwise employed as assistant managers to Walter Smith and they had a game that weekend. Tommy invited me to Rangers' training complex at Murray Park, just a short drive from my house in Lambhill and it is an offer I must take up, just for the fun of it.

Kenny, Ally and Tommy might just try and get me to educate the Rangers midfield on some of the darker arts of the game – it could be filmed and put out as some kind of X-rated certificate training video. My old adversary Mr Souness would doubtlessly approve.

Big 'Basil Fawlty' - Peter Godfrey - bounded over with hand outstretched. Nothing had changed – a really nice guy who still had this almost innocent Forrest Gump air about him. Either that, or it was the combination of his huge smile - although the 'tache was long gone - and impenetrable Grangemouth accent. 'Basil' and I were soon joined by two others of the defensive unit of that 1987 team – Dibble and Neil Cooper. Sadly, illness had prevented Tony from making it and he was sorely missed, as were the two Franks, Luther and Macca. However, it was just magical – almost everyone from my past playing days was there and I was fit and sober, able to enjoy the occasion and take it all in.

At full-time, the St Mirren legends were led onto the pitch to say farewell to Love Street and the fans for one last time. The place was rocking with noise and there was a degree of confusion as instructions on what to do were almost impossible to understand. I knew that we were to go out onto the pitch, so ambled onwards, carrying on a conversation with Jimmy Bone. When he didn't answer, I looked round to find that he was 30 yards back with the rest of the players.

Like a scene out of Cocoon, they were ambling forward at a snail's pace and I was standing in the middle of the pitch on my own, feeling like the proverbial spare part. Phil Clarke, the PA announcer was clearly struggling with his emotions and was shouting into the microphone, the end result being a strange noise that came out of the battered old PA system. He beckoned me over.

'Me?'

'Aye, Aber – you.' He handed me the microphone. Bloody Hell, I thought, this wasn't part of the plan.

I looked around for help, stuck for something to say. I saw 'Starsky', an accomplished public speaker, who had performed amazingly when delivering the eulogy in the high emotion of Tommy Burns' funeral. Surely he could help. He was laughing his face off, with the unmistakeable message that I was on my own. S**t. My mind went blank. What can I say?

Then I heard it. 'Aber's Gonnae Get Ye!'

Louder. 'Aber's Gonnae Get Ye!'

Louder still. All four stands belting it out – 'Aber's Gonnae Get Ye!'

I wasn't trying to work the crowd – I was actually almost overcome with emotion. After everything I had been through, this was like the final crowning moment that rubber-stamped the comeback and all in front of my old pals and colleagues.

In an instant, I relaxed and thought - Billy, you'll never get a chance like this again – so just enjoy it. As opposed to Phil's manic shouting, but who could blame him, I decided just to speak quietly and clearly, so that the message had half a chance of being heard.

'Hello there. It's a shame we dropped two points today, but it's the end of an era and the start of a new one. All the best to Gus and the boys for the rest of the season and a Happy New Year to the rest of you. Aber is back.'

The ovation was massive and if I was made of lesser stuff, I would have probably started greetin', right in the middle of the centre circle of the place that had become my second home, in the final match to be played there before it was demolished.

It was the closest I've come to shedding a tear on any football pitch, but what a way to end my time at the ground. For the final time, Love Street reverberated to the sound of 'Aber's Gonnae Get Ye'

And they're absolutely right.

Billy Abercromby 2009

ABER'S GONNAE GET YE!

Aber's ~~Ocean's~~ Eleven

TONY FITZPATRICK

a.k.a 'Fitzy' or 'Tony the Tank'
St Mirren FC 1973 – 1988
536 Appearances
St Mirren FC Manager 1988-1991, 1996-1998

BILLY and I went to the same school and although I was two years ahead of him, I knew him pretty well and was more than aware of his footballing abilities from the playground and the school teams, which also included many guys who went on to have successful careers, most notably Charlie Nicholas. I was already on the books at St Mirren when Alex Ferguson signed him and I knew straight away that he was going to make the grade.

Aber was a great guy for me to play alongside in midfield – I always got plenty of room to play my game as the opposition players seemed to be strangely wary of him. However, simply labelling Billy as a hard man didn't do him justice. Make no mistake, he was a very, very good footballer and one of the best passers of a ball that you could hope to see.

He also had an almost unique talent of being the best stand up tackler I have ever seen. Most players commit to a tackle by sliding or lunging in, but Billy had the knack of being able to stand up to an opponent, thus keeping his own balance and composure while a seemingly elastic leg would win the ball and get a killer pass away in the blink of an eye. This is a talent that was probably only truly appreciated by those in the game, but it was vital to the success of the St Mirren teams that we played in.

It was said that he was a yard short of pace - I faced the same criticism as well - and this counted against him getting more International honours, but this makes me laugh. He was a supremely fit player and I don't remember too many opponents running away from him. If they did manage to do so, they certainly didn't second time round.

He was one of those players who gave everything to the cause and it was easy to see why the supporters idolised him. Feared on the pitch, but extremely affable off it, you could see the natural rapport he had with the fans and very few people had a bad word to say about him.

My fondest memory of Billy was in the immediate aftermath of the full-time whistle going at Hampden in 1987, as we started to make our way towards the main stand steps to collect the trophy. Billy was the captain, but he turned round to me and said: 'Go on Tony – you go up and get it.' I know that we had been through so much together, but for him to even consider passing up the greatest moment of his career so that I could benefit - well, it speaks volumes about him as a man. Of course I declined, but I have never forgotten that moment.

I know Billy's family well and occasionally bumped into him when his life seemed to be hurtling towards a tragic end. I hurt for Billy and his family back then, but I am so genuinely delighted that he is well on the way to a comeback. It took real courage and inner fighting ability to conquer his demons and rebuild his life, but anyone who knows the real Billy Abercromby would never bet against him achieving his aims.

Aber's Ocean's Eleven

BILLY STARK

a.k.a 'Starsky'
St Mirren FC 1975-1983

I SIGNED for St Mirren in 1975 and soon found myself in the first team, along with Frank McGarvey and Tony Fitzpatrick as Fergie set about establishing a team of youthful endeavour and skill. In the summer of 1976 we went out to the West Indies on a pre-season tour and I clearly remembered that Aber was along for that trip, despite only being signed a few weeks previously by Sir Alex – he had clearly been earmarked for a bright future by Fergie.

The following decade was a truly great period for St Mirren with a series of great teams evolving at Love Street. There was a whole host of excellent players spread through each of the sides that were built - Frank McGarvey, Tony Fitzpatrick, Bobby Reid, Peter Weir, Doug Somner, Frank McDougall, Frank McAvennie, Ian Scanlon to name but a few. All were marvellous players and a privilege to play with. However, there was one player who was there for the entire decade and I am sure that I am not just speaking for myself when I say that a large part of how the above players and myself were able to shine, was entirely due to the work and unique skills of Billy Abercromby.

In many ways, Aber was ahead of his time, with his specialised role of the defensive midfielder/distributor being quite rare in that era of football in comparison to its popularity within the modern game. Football in the late 70s and 80s was awash with plenty of ball winners, but very few knew how to play football once the ball was won.

Tackling is an art, often unappreciated by the casual observer, but Aber was a master – as opposed to myself. Allied to his timing, he had an incredible flexibility and without wanting to sound too dodgy, the span of his groin was incredible - you could be sure that you had beaten him with a bit of skill, sending him the wrong way, yet somehow his leg would elongate and stretch out to make the seemingly impossible tackle. And then a killer pass would be delivered – and that is what makes the real difference.

As well as the above attributes, Billy could always be relied on to pop up with a crucial goal. I don't remember Aber scoring many, but when he did, they usually mattered in important ties. For example, he scored the winner in our 2-1 win over Elfsborg, in Sweden. It was St Mirren's first-ever European tie and as is often the way with the media, Elfsborg were dismissed as 'some team from Sweden'. This did them a great disservice as they were a very, very good team, who made us work extremely hard for the 0-0 in Paisley that saw us through - and technically ensured that Billy Abercromby had scored the winner in Saints' first ever European tie.

In a dressing room full of some pretty off the wall characters, Aber stood out on his own. Always smiling and with a quite laid-back, affable manner that was at complete odds to his on-pitch persona, he was a great team-mate to have around. He never took himself too seriously and God help anyone who did.

To be the captain of a St Mirren Scottish Cup Winning side is a very rare honour and for Aber to be assured of this legendary status is very well-deserved.

ABER'S GONNAE GET YE!

Aber's Ocean's Eleven

FRANK McDOUGALL

a.k.a 'Luther'
St Mirren FC 1979 – 1984

ABER was any professional player's dream team-mate. A great engine, with superb fitness levels, a superb passer of the ball and an astonishingly strong and accurate - when he wanted to be - tackler. I played with some great players at Love Street – Tony Fitzpatrick, Billy Stark, Peter Weir, Ian Scanlon, but it was Aber who was the driving force that allowed them to express their talents.

In a reflection of the St Mirren teams of that era, Aber feared no opponent irrespective of reputation. Two examples of this summed Billy up perfectly:

When we were playing St Etienne, Aber was asked to mark Larios and 'Cowboy' McCormack got the job of marking Platini. It was a thankless task as this big fella Larios seemed unstoppable, but Aber kept trying to stop him in his tracks. It was fruitless as Billy simply bounced of the big man's body. At half-time Billy managed to raise a smile when, as most would have asked to be subbed to spare more punishment, he calmly announced: 'He's no' bad – but I'll get him in the end.'

Also, I got my leg badly broken in a Scottish Cup tie against Celtic following a late tackle by Danny McGrain, who had been a big hero of mine and Billy's. To make matters worse, I was fined by the SFA for comments I made about the tackle to a newspaper while still in plaster - fined more than Danny was when the tackle was made and initially there were fears for my career. Despite his admiration for Danny as a player, Billy took up his own mission of seeking retribution for me. In the side's next league clash at Love Street, Danny McGrain was stretchered off inside 15 minutes.

Socially, he was great fun in a dressing-room packed full of characters. Most of the tales are not for public consumption, but as Paisley's Rat Pack we had a lot of fun in an era when it was easier for top level pros to let their hair down.

Aber was at the centre of a group of guys who would test the patience of any manager – Macca, 'Cowboy', Aber and myself – we were like the Four Musketeers. Great days that I will remember all my life.

Billy Abercromby – great player, team-mate and friend. Crap snooker player. I'll give you a 146 start, Aber.

ABER'S GONNAE GET YE!

Aber's Ocean's Eleven

RICKY McFARLANE

a.k.a 'The Brain'
St Mirren FC Physio, Assistant Manager and Manager 1976 – 1984

BILLY was an all-round player and there was way more to his game than just the physical aspect which he is often remembered for. It has always been my belief that if he had that fabled extra yard of pace he would have been a top, top player, at the highest level in football. He would certainly have been a regular in the full international set-up for Scotland and would have played for one of the major clubs, either side of the border.

He had such a laid-back attitude, that unlike many who passed up such opportunities, Billy could have handled playing for one of the major clubs without any bother at all. It was to St Mirren's benefit that so many teams were prejudicial towards him because of this perceived lack of pace. They were overlooking one Hell of a player.

Billy was an intelligent lad, with a great awareness of the game. He listened to tactical discussions and could easily analyse and understand what we were trying to achieve as a team. He was an excellent technical player and I also remember when he first arrived at Love Street that he was a superb dribbler with the ball, regularly going past three or four players at a time.

His other main strength was mental toughness and no matter how cruel the disappointment - and there were a few - Billy could be guaranteed to bounce back and was a great example to all his team mates.

People often look back on that era and remark, correctly, on some of the wonderful players St Mirren had - Tony Fitzpatrick, Lex Richardson, Billy Stark, Frank McGarvey and Frank McAvennie to name but a few. They all had one thing in common – Billy Abercromby. He did the hard work that let them play. I thought Aber was terrific and crucial to the success enjoyed by St Mirren during my time at the club.

I may be a physio, but Billy Abercromby was a study in psychology.

Aber's Ocean's Eleven

JOHN McCORMACK

a.k.a 'Cowboy'
St Mirren FC 1980-1984

BILLY was one of these guys who enjoyed life to the full and that cheeky grin was never far from his face. On the pitch was a different story. Fully-committed would be the best description and it was no different whether playing or training. Team-mate or rival, Aber didn't care – if you were in the way, then too bad.

At one point Aber started to get a reputation within the game that was putting the wind up the opposition that he was so committed he was even doing his own team-mates. In actual fact, this was true. During one high-tempo practice match at training, he managed to put someone out injured for about six weeks. On another occasion he and Jackie Copland- the most experienced pro at the club - had a stand up fight. Crazy days indeed and I am pretty sure that Billy and I had one or two major altercations as well. But Billy knew only one way to play and it was all part and parcel of the game.

My favourite memory of Billy during my days at Love Street was when he and Alex Beckett bowled in for training one morning, clearly the worse for wear. To be honest, they were completely p****d and it was 10am.

'Me and Becky have had a baby,' proclaimed Aber to the stunned dressing room. Alex had indeed become a father the night before and it hadn't taken Billy long to wet/soak the baby's head with his team-mate.

Somehow we managed to get the pair of them into their training gear and set out for the usual few laps of the pitch to get warmed up. This was proving a major problem for the pair of them, but we managed to keep them boxed in with the pack as we lapped the pitch, pushing, shoving and propping them up as we ran.

So far so good as Ricky McFarlane hadn't worked out what was going on. It didn't last long, as the next drill involved some crosses being fired in to the box. Billy and Alex were, as normal, selected as crossers and as each time they ran to meet a pass to cross in, only managed to fall over in a heap as they kicked fresh air. The game was up. I think Ricky calmed down a few days later.

ABER'S GONNAE GET YE!

Aber's Ocean's Eleven

LEX RICHARDSON
a.k.a 'Lexy'
St Mirren FC 1975 - 1983

BILLY and I had a tremendous time together at St Mirren, both on and off the pitch. It was a dressing room full of characters, some of them Saints on the pitch, but definitely not off it. At the core of the high jinks was a group of players - Aber, Alex Beckett, Frank McDougall and myself.

Thursday was our special day and straight after training we would head up to a snooker club near Charing Cross, in Glasgow that 'Luther' was a member of. We'd stay there all afternoon, before heading off to the dogs at Shawfield. After a few more hours of unwinding, we'd round off the evening with a few nightcaps in Glasgow City Centre. Looking back, this was fairly ludicrous behaviour for professional footballers, but for us it was the norm and the game was so much different from how it is today.

What countered this was the fact that we were ferocious trainers - something that put us in good stead for the rest of our careers, probably allowing us to indulge more than we ought to when not playing, but still deliver the goods when it mattered on the pitch.

Some of the tours that we used to go on with St Mirren - I could write a book about them myself, but it would never get printed for legal reasons. I remember Billy going missing for 48 hours in Brazil and he reappeared out of nowhere with very little recollection of where he had been, or who he had been with for the previous two days. He just laughed it off, gave a wee shrug and casually got on with playing, as if nothing had happened.

He was some boy, Aber and had a wonderful love of life. I was happy to share his philosophy of having a good time – all the time. The trouble was, it probably did affect our careers to some extent.

The St Mirren sides of the late 1970s and early 80s were excellent, especially the 1979/80 team that won the Anglo-Scottish Cup and should have won the Premier League. Many people focus on our poor run in the last three games, but forget the fact that we didn't start playing properly until October, giving everyone else eight games of a start.

Considering this, you'd have thought that there would have been more international recognition for our players. Many, like Billy and myself got call-ups for the Under-21s, but it never went any further – and I think I know why.

Within Scottish football, the St Mirren team had a well-deserved degree of notoriety for playing hard and partying even harder. Jock Stein was running the entire international set-up and had a huge influence on the players being selected for the Under-21 team as well.

Big Jock knew everything - and I mean everything - that was going on with the players in or around his selection plans. He had spies everywhere and the off-the-pitch antics of the Saints players would certainly have been brought to his attention and that of the SFA hierarchy.

There were certain things that were no-nos and we were blatantly not playing the game. For example, I had just scored two goals at Ibrox and Arthur Montford came into the dressing room to see if I wanted to come on Scotsport later to talk about the goals. The general rule was that you said yes, took the £50 fee and tried not to get dazzled by Arthur's latest sports jacket under the studio lights.

That time and any other time Billy or I were asked to do the show, we just said: 'No. Sorry Arthur, we're away out on the town the night.' It seems trivial, but it was just another anecdotal piece of evidence against the Saints crew that would add to the growing bad boys reputation.

Frank McDougall was one of the most lethal finishers seen in Scottish football, yet he hardly got a look-in on the Scotland scene. While I got some media attention and accolades for my attacking midfield play, I was also recognised within the game to be about the fittest player in Scottish football.

Again, I got a couple of Under-21 caps against West Germany and England, but that was it. As for Aber – his one Under-21 cap was scant recognition for a player who was respected and feared in equal measure by every team he ever faced.

I don't regret any of it, as I had such a good time on and off the field and as Aber would put it – life's too short. And he almost proved that himself. A truly great friend, player and colleague, I am certain that Billy's mischievous grin will be around for some time yet.

Aber's Ocean's Eleven

STEVE CLARKE
a.k.a. 'Stevie Boy'
St Mirren FC 1979-1986

I JOINED St Mirren as a raw youngster, ever so slightly apprehensive of coming into a dressing room full of 'difficult' players. The Saints squad of that time were notorious for their off-the-field activities, in what was a completely different culture from that found in professional football nowadays.

Billy Abercromby was already in the class of seasoned pro, despite the fact he was only in his early 20s and immediately he came across as a strong character. Definitely a ring-leader of the hard core of characters that ran the dressing room.

However, he always seemed to keep an eye out for me and was like some kind of protective big brother. Whenever there was a players' evening out - and there were quite a few - he always seemed to be on hand to guide me to the door if it looked like I was beginning to fall behind the pace set by him and his trusty lieutenants such as Frank McAvennie and Lex Richardson.

I recall one pre-season tour to the Isle of Man where a serious night out was being planned by the usual suspects and Aber took time out to have a wee word with me. He was dead set against me going out with the gang and could see that I was a vulnerable young player whose potential may not be best served if spending too long following the less than perfect example being set by Aber and his very Merry Men.

It may sound strange, but I have always appreciated this and his quiet way of looking out for me definitely helped me get established at Love Street and develop as a player.

On the pitch, Aber was a true leader. Always quiet on the field, he let his actions do the talking and many an opponent felt the full force of his quiet ways. If it was a difficult game you could always rely on Aber to quite literally fight our corner and this was an inspiration to his team mates.

On a personal level, if I wasn't having a good game Billy would always come over and offer words of encouragement - never criticism - and again, this is something I remember fondly and appreciate to this day.

Technically, he was a superb player, something often overlooked as people focused on his competitive edge. He had one particular trick, where he could beat a man with ease dribbling with the ball. The thing was, Aber didn't exactly have pace to burn, so I couldn't fathom out how he was able to do it, until after I had left Love Street.

Looking at some old footage, I could then see that Billy had mastered a skill of being able to quickly lift the ball over the foot of a defender who was trying to tackle him. This was done while on the move and with the outside of his boot, all the while in complete control of the ball. It is a very hard skill to master and execute, particularly in the professional ranks and I found it quite amazing and remarkable.

Perhaps it is some testament to his talents that I still refer this piece of skill to young players under my charge in the English Premiership. Aber is still making his mark to this day.

JIMMY BONE

a.k.a 'Papa'
St Mirren FC 1978-1982
Assistant Manager 1986-1988
Manager 1992-1996

ON the pitch, Billy Abercromby was one of the most technically gifted players of his generation, something that was often overlooked on account of his hard man image - although he could be a dirty wee bugger as well. Ball retention, distribution, tackling, reading of a game, stamina – Aber had it all and he was a real joy to both play beside and coach.

He always had real leadership qualities, not necessarily shouting at players, but more by setting a fighting example with his actions on the field of play and always finding time to have a wee quiet word with colleagues when it looked like they may need it.

When Alex Smith and I came into Love Street in late 1986, we found a rudderless team, with Tony out injured and Aber serving a then world-record ban. I told Alex that if we could keep Billy under control off the pitch, then he would make a great captain. Alex agreed and Billy never let us down. Within months he went on to be only the third man in history to captain a Scottish Cup winning team for St Mirren.

However, that 1987 team was nowhere near as good a team as the one where Billy and I first joined up in 1978. Indeed, in my honest opinion, St Mirren would have won the league in 1980 had Bobby Reid - as good a player, if not better, than Willie Miller - not been injured.

As it was, I was proud to captain the Saints team that became the first Scottish team to win the Anglo-Scottish Cup, which at the time was no mean feat. Nottingham Forest had won it two or three years previously and by the time we won it, Forest were playing in European Finals.

Aber was a young player, forging his career among a squad of excellent pros. To maintain his place he had to perform consistently at a high level, week in week out. It was the making of him as a player. This consistency became his trademark and I can honestly count on the fingers of one hand the number of poor games Billy had.

Off the pitch, Billy was a complete bomb scare. He was great company and had a philosophy of anything goes – and it often did. He was very hard to dislike and his casual, cheery approach to life was infectious. It was also at complete odds with his on-pitch persona of a quiet, brooding, lethal, midfield enforcer. He was also a clever guy and extremely sharp – not just in the tackle. When the rightly-feared Graeme Souness once threatened to sort him out, Billy's response was a casual shrug, followed by: 'I don't see anyone holding you back.'

The one problem Billy had was that he was easily bored and I have no doubt that the terrible injury he suffered at Tromso and the subsequent 12-month plus spent on the sidelines was a huge factor in drink getting a real hold of him and he was never the same player again. From what I then began to hear on the grapevine, it was almost to lead to his death.

However, Billy is mentally and physically resilient and I was not surprised to hear that he defied the medical odds to complete a remarkable comeback. 'Aber's Gonnae Get Ye' was the rallying cry of the St Mirren fans and that is so true of Billy's never-say-die attitude. He'll be around for a long while yet – so, watch out!

ABER'S GONNAE GET YE!

Aber's ~~Ocean's~~ Eleven

ALEX SMITH

a.k.a. 'Faither'
Manager, St Mirren FC 1986-1988

BILLY Abercromby always had such strong inner strength, both physically and mentally, that it has come as no surprise to me that he is winning his battle with his demons. Billy was always a winner – a fierce competitor with a drive and intelligence that was often unappreciated.

When I arrived at Love Street, Billy was in the middle of serving a huge ban, for which he had also been fined by the SFA, fined by his own club, stripped of the captaincy and placed on the transfer list. He was very, very depressed.

After one of my first training sessions, I called him over and asked if he was injured, completely forgetting about the infamous events against Motherwell a few weeks previously. Instead of being annoyed, Billy simply cracked a wry smile and said: 'No - not injured, Boss. Banned.' I asked him to come into my office and tell me all about what had happened. As far as I was concerned, it was a one-off explosion of misplaced strength and aggression – usually directed effectively against opposing players, not referees.

The lad was hurting badly. Football and St Mirren was his life. I felt the punishments by the SFA were draconian enough, without St Mirren feeling the need to put the boot in as well. I went to see the chairman and although he was unhappy about it, I persuaded him to allow me to suspend the huge fine imposed on Billy by the club. Any more problems and the fine would be re-applied. There were never to be any more problems. My assistant, Jimmy Bone was an old playing colleague of Billy's and he had assured me that if I handled Billy right, he would never let me down. He was right.

We got Billy fit again, which wasn't a problem as he was a very, very good trainer. Tony Fitzpatrick was out with a long-term injury and I had no doubts who I wanted as captain. I wanted to re-instate Billy. The board of directors along with many others were astonished. They strongly stated that Billy didn't have the right image for the club. Tony was the image they were after. Well, Tony was injured and I'll say this with some degree of knowledge and certainty - if Billy Abercromby had not been in the side, especially as captain, St Mirren would not have won the Scottish Cup in 1987.

Billy could run a game. Players know the best players – not just the most skilful, but also the brave ones. Brave enough to face up to the opposition's hard men and take the battle to them. Billy was a natural leader for the team.

The younger players in the team looked up to him and he also roused the fighting spirit of the squad. In particular, Kenny McDowall and Ian Ferguson sparked off him. It was a team full of great players like Ian Ferguson, Campbell Money and Tony Fitzpatrick - whose appearance in the Final was often overlooked for its importance as he did a great job that day. But the driving force of the team was Billy Abercromby.

The following season Billy had started with a worsening Achilles 'problem. It was getting worse by the game, but Billy knew we needed him and went along with the medical treatment to ensure he was available each week. An operation was imminent, but first of all we needed to get through an awkward second leg tie against Tromso.

'Just one more game Aber,' I pleaded with him and out he went again. His Achilles' ruptured after 15 minutes and he would never play for St Mirren again. It probably curtailed his career at the top level. It was a very sorry way for such a magnificent career at Love Street to end.

It was a pleasure working with Billy and he richly deserves his legendary status amongst the St Mirren fans, who could also recognise that aside from the bad boy reputation, Billy Abercromby was one Hell of a player.

ABER'S GONNAE GET YE!

~~Aber's~~ ~~Ocean's~~ Eleven

DEREK HAMILTON

a.k.a. 'Moon Man'
St Mirren FC 1983 – 1988

THE day I signed for St Mirren from Aberdeen in 1983 will always be etched on my mind. Leaving Pittodrie after five years, I was a wee bit nervous of going to a new dressing-room. As I met the players, I shook Aber's hand and immediately felt some kind of weird connection. I just knew that this guy was as much of a headcase as myself and that we were going to have a lot of fun and games. I had no idea how right I was to be.

In the final league game before the 1987 Final, I injured my ankle at Ibrox. I was distraught, as my cup final appearance was in danger. I could hardly walk, let alone run.

On the Monday down at Seamill, club doctor, Stuart McCormack put something like seven injections into my ankle and Alex Smith watched as I started to run around the training pitch. 'Great, Derek – but can you kick a ball?' I promptly chipped a ball into his hands from 40 yards away. 'OK - you're in.' I nearly cried.

A few days later in the Hampden dressing room, Stuart once again started using my ankle as some kind of medical dartboard. I was lying on the physio's table with needles sticking out of my ankle when Aber strolled past. 'What's up with you, ya big Jessie,' he said. 'C'mon – we've got a game to win.' And win we did – the greatest day in my life other than the birth of my child.

As a team mate, Billy was invaluable and his fearsome reputation was well-deserved and much appreciated by his colleagues. If anyone tried to push us about, we just knew that they were making a big mistake.

Two games against Rangers highlighted this perfectly. In one game at Ibrox, Rangers striker John MacDonald had been involved in a few controversial moments and we were all raging. As a corner came in, Campbell Money collected it and ushered us all up the park before he cleared it. As I was jogging up the pitch, I heard Aber say: 'Check out MacDonald.' I turned round and saw the man known as 'Polaris' staggering out of the box with blood flowing from a burst nose. I looked round at Billy and he just gave me a cheeky wink.

In these days of multi-angle camera shots, he would have been done for assault by the SFA, but back then he was just evening up the score – and few complaints were made.

In a game against Rangers, at Love Street we thought Billy would finally meet his match in the shape of Graeme Souness. The two were soon at it hammer and tongs and it finally blew up when Aber went in late on Ian Durrant, whom Souness was protecting in the Rangers midfield.

Souness was threatening Billy with all sorts, but Aber just smiled and kept steaming through Souness at every opportunity. Souness was going mental, shouting his mouth off at Aber. Just more wee smiles. This was what Aber was so good at - he could get right inside the head of opponents and that is what would often win the battle, not just the physical stuff.

When Souness eventually subbed himself, he shouted over: 'I'll f*****g see you at Ibrox, Abercromby.' Billy just laughed and waved him off the pitch. Few could claim to have come out on top against Souness – Billy was one of that select group.

Everyone used to remark that he was so unflappable, but he did have one weak spot - Rennies heartburn pills. He was obsessed about necking a couple before a game to avoid heartburn and even used to carry a spare tablet in the top of his sock.

Before one game at Love Street, he became frantic – he'd forgotten them. Like some kind of drug addict panicking about their lost stash, Aber was pacing around like a madman. 'I need my Rennie's,' he shouted. The rest of us were trying not to laugh and in the end, when he was seemingly on the point of breakdown, Norrie McWhirter went out to a local shop to get supplies.

ABER'S GONNAE GET YE!

When Norrie came back with the goods he was treated like a Golden Child by Aber, who was now ready for action. Drug Dependency? Hardly – but it shows you how daft players can get about superstitions. Mr.Cool was no different.

Off the park, we were inseparable – something that maybe didn't do either of us much good. I introduced him to exotic cocktails like flaming Sambuccas, which just about killed him the first time he tried them. Spending too long posing with the blazing glass, when he eventually knocked back the drink, the heat of the glass meant it stuck to his face, sending hot green fluid all over the rest of his face. He saw the funny side once the burns healed.

On another occasion in The Cotton Club, in Paisley, I ordered 26 Sambuccas for the pair of us. As the young barman started lighting them, the manager said we were only to get four each, which was hardly helping, to be honest. What made us laugh was the suggestion that they were worried about the possibility of us being a fire risk - just ask anyone about fire and The Cotton Club which burned down.

Soon the booze buddies routine began to get out of control, from sleeping under the pool table in the Ring o' Bells, in Elderslie during a daytime Diamond White promotion, to crashing into the gates of the Rockfield Hotel as we arrived for a pre-match meal. We often drove together from our houses in Beith and Lochwinnoch - a dangerous enough route without us at the wheel.

But the one incident that summed up the madness, involved a night out near Aber's old stomping ground in Maryhill. I drove up there and parked outside a pub. As per the plan, we got blootered – no surprises there. In the morning, the car wasn't where I'd left it. I had no memory of leaving the pub, but deep down suspected that this might not be a theft. I had to go down to England for a few days and came straight to Maryhill on my way back, still looking for the car. I found it straight away - parked at an angle just a few yards down the road from a Police Station. As I got closer, I could see that there was still a beef curry takeaway on the dashboard and one of my shoes in the footwell. I was right – it wasn't theft. Just a typical night out with Aber.

A great guy, good friend and colleague with the heart of a lion. Aber was a one-off – they don't make them like that any more.

Aber's Ocean's Eleven

FRANK McAVENNIE

a.k.a. 'Macca'
St Mirren FC 1980 – 1985 , 1994

THE Saints teams of the early 1980s were a bunch of nutcases off the field and had a well-deserved notorious reputation for our off-the-park antics, but by Christ, could we play on the pitch as well. Frank McDougall, Lex Richardson, Tony Fitzpatrick, Ian Scanlon, Billy Stark - and myself naturally - all thrived in the team and we could hold our own against any team in the land, playing some great attacking football that the Paisley public really took to. However, without the spadework of Billy Abercromby, we would have been nothing.

Aber was the first genuine holding midfielder that is now so prevalent in the modern game. Plenty of teams had ball-winners, but most couldn't actually play. Make no mistake - Billy could play. He was also easily the hardest tackler I ever played with or witnessed on the field of play – truly ferocious and fair – most of the time - and he was definitely feared by opposition teams.

It sounds simple - get the ball off the opposition and give it to the players who can hurt them. Actually executing both of these on a consistent level at the top of the professional game – well, that is another matter. When I was at West Ham, Neil Orr was asked to do the same job. Neil was a good pro and he did the task OK, but I knew that Aber was streets ahead of him. Aber would have shone in the English top flight.

Perhaps not as good a player as Roy Keane, but in my humble opinion, every bit the equal of Michael Essien. The mind boggles as to how much he would have earned in the modern game.......... and what kind of partying that would have brought.

St Mirren fans should never ever forget Billy's loyalty to the club and it is no coincidence that he was the one player who was at Love Street throughout a hugely successful decade of football at the club. That is unlikely to ever be repeated.

Off the park, Billy was a great guy and had an infectious love of life, which equated well with my own outlook. At that time, I was single and known as a bit of a party boy and some of my colleagues used to use me as cover if they went off on a disappearing act from the marital home. This didn't bother me – as long as they remembered to tell me.

The one time he went out on an all-night session using me as an excuse, Aber never remembered to tell me about the Macca Alibi and I had to draw on all my skills for telling wee black and white lies out of the blue when his wife appeared at my house looking for him. To use Frank McAvennie as a cover story to bail you out of trouble - now that is the definition of having a wild night out.

My favourite memory of Aber's crazy ways was one night when we were having a players' night out at the Warehouse club, in Glasgow. As we all began partying the night away, it was soon clear that one of the main movers of the gang was missing – Aber. A short while later he appeared, dressed in a sheepskin jacket and carpet slippers. Hardly nightclubbing gear, but I guess the bouncers were just as wary of him as opposition players. Anyway, as he casually strolled through the club towards us, cutting a dash in his unique attire, with a huge smile on his face, the reason for the strange appearance was relayed:

'I was out walking the dog and I realised I forgot about the night out, so I legged it straight here.'

'Where's the dug?' he was asked.

'Oh, I put it on the bus home and told the driver to let it off at the next stop. It can work its way home from there. Pint of lager please, Macca.'

On a serious level, as much as he loved a good time, Aber was deadly serious on the pitch. He was a bit special and he was a winner. I have no doubts that he'll win his battle with alcohol – it's just another opponent to be beaten. All the best, Billy – you're a legend.

Thanks To...

Bill Ross
Yvonne Farlow
Carol Mungai
Gerry Docherty
Bill Leckie
Alan Provan
Campbell Kennedy
Al Mitchell
Everybuddie on blackandwhitearmy.com
and last but not least - the Big Man in the sky.

Note From The Co-Author

I WAS a fan and I now consider myself a friend. The life and career of Billy Abercromby had always been a very interesting story to put it mildly. By early 2007, it looked like there would be no happy ending, but with trademark determination Aber fought back from the brink.

Being asked to help with his autobiography was easy to accept. Billy was simply the cult hero for a generation of Saints fans and there was a genuine connection between Aber and the St Mirren supporters, especially during the games, when he would right wrongs and fight the cause with an inspiring combination of skill and aggression.

Simply, Billy Abercromby was the living embodiment of the Saints fans out on the pitch and we loved him. It was fitting that it was Billy who would lift the Scottish Cup in 1987, but what happened to him almost immediately after this era-defining moment certainly wasn't in the script.

This is for my late father Ronnie, who took me to Love Street to watch the Fergie Revolution and for my son, Cameron, for whom I hope to do something similar.

Fraser Kirkwood, 2009